The Soviet Union
and Strategic Arms

Also of Interest

France, the Soviet Union, and the Nuclear Weapons Issue, Robbin F. Laird

Soviet Allies: The Warsaw Pact and the Issue of Reliability, Daniel N. Nelson

†*Thinking About National Security: Defense and Foreign Policy in a Dangerous World,* Harold Brown

National Security and Technology Transfer: The Strategic Dimensions of East-West Trade, edited by Gary K. Bertsch and John R. McIntyre

Laser Weapons in Space: Policy and Doctrine, edited by Keith B. Payne

The Soviet Art of War: Doctrine, Strategy, and Tactics, edited by Harriet Fast Scott and William F. Scott

†*The Armed Forces of the USSR,* Third Edition, Revised and Updated, Harriet Fast Scott and William F. Scott

Nuclear Deterrence in U.S.-Soviet Relations, Keith B. Payne

†*Arms Control and International Security,* edited by Roman Kolkowicz and Neil Joeck

Soviet Politics in the 1980s, edited by Helmut Sonnenfeldt

Soviet Nuclear Weapons Policy: A Research Guide, William C. Green

†*The Defense of the West: Strategic and European Security Issues Reappraised,* edited by Robert Kennedy and John M. Weinstein

Military Strategy in Transition: Defense and Deterrence in the 1980s, edited by Keith A. Dunn and William O. Staudenmaier

The MX Decision: A New Direction in Weapons Procurement Policy? Lauren H. Holland and Robert A. Hoover

Strategic and Critical Materials, L. Harold Bullis and James E. Mielke

†Available in hardcover and paperback.

A Westview Special Study

The Soviet Union and Strategic Arms
Robbin F. Laird and Dale R. Herspring

This book provides the student of Soviet affairs, international security, and arms control issues with a comprehensive overview of the role of strategic nuclear weapons in Soviet military and foreign policy. It focuses primarily on an assessment of Soviet policy and perspectives since 1970—the period of strategic parity. Drs. Laird and Herspring concentrate on three themes. They argue first that the Soviets believe the strategic relationship with the United States is forged around the reality of mutual assured destruction; second, that although Soviet leaders have accepted this objective reality, they have nevertheless attempted to build a military force that could defeat the United States in war without resorting to strategic nuclear weapons; and finally, that the Soviets consider strategic parity with the United States to be the cornerstone of their military and diplomatic competition with the United States. The authors discuss the Soviet concept of strategic parity in terms both of Soviet perceptions of the U.S. challenge and of their bargaining behavior in arms control negotiations with the United States. The book concludes with an assessment of the future of the strategic arms race. The authors' contention that an open-ended and dangerously unregulated arms race might well be unleashed is, as Zbigniew Brzezinski says in his foreword to the book, "a warning that gives their book not only great analytical salience but direct policy relevance."

Robbin F. Laird is an analyst for the Center for Naval Analyses, Alexandria, Virginia. Dr. Laird has coauthored (with Erik Hoffmann) *The Politics of Economic Modernization in the Soviet Union* (1982), *The "Scientific-Technological Revolution" and Soviet Foreign Policy* (1982), and *Technocratic Socialism* (forthcoming), and coedited (with Erik Hoffmann) *The Soviet Polity in the Modern Era* (1984). He has a forthcoming book with Westview Press entitled *France, the Soviet Union, and the Nuclear Weapons Issue*.

Dale R. Herspring is the author of *East German Civil-Military Relations: The Impact of Technology, 1949–1972* (1973) and coeditor (with Ivan Volgyes) of *Civil-Military Relations in Communist Systems* (Westview, 1978). He is a career foreign service officer with the U.S. Department of State and has served abroad in U.S. embassies in Warsaw and Moscow, as well as in Washington, D.C., at the department and at the Pentagon, where he was a state-defense exchange officer. Dr. Herspring is an adjunct professor in the Department of Government in the Russian area studies program at Georgetown University.

The Soviet Union and Strategic Arms

Robbin F. Laird
and Dale R. Herspring

Foreword by Zbigniew Brzezinski

Westview Press / Boulder and London

To
Marc Gilbert and Murray Marder

A Westview Special Study

Copyright © 1984 by Westview Press, Inc.

Published in 1984 in the United States of America by Westview Press, Inc., 5500 Central Avenue, Boulder, Colorado 80301; Frederick A. Praeger, Publisher

Library of Congress Cataloging in Publication Data
Laird, Robbin F. (Robbin Frederick), 1946–
    The Soviet Union and strategic arms.
    (A Westview special study)
    Includes bibliographies.
    1. Soviet Union—Military policy. 2. Strategic
forces—Soviet Union. 3. Deterrence (Strategy)
4. Atomic weapons and disarmament. I. Herspring,
Dale R. (Dale Roy) II. Title.
UA770.L333 1984   355'.0335'47   84-15221
ISBN 0-8133-0054-1
ISBN 0-8133-0151-3 (pbk.)

Printed and bound in the United States of America

10   9   8   7   6   5   4   3   2   1

Contents

Tables

Foreword

Robbin F. Laird and Dale R. Herspring, in their joint book, address a centrally important question: What is the character of the Soviet nuclear challenge and what does it portend for U.S.-Soviet relations? With the rise of the Soviet Union to strategic parity with the United States, and with the U.S. president even unilaterally conceding in public that the Soviet Union is strategically superior, this question is central to a proper understanding and management of the U.S.-Soviet relationship.

The answer that the two authors provide in their exhaustive, highly researched, and systematically argued volume reinforces the conclusion that I reached on the basis of my four years' experience in the White House. Unlike President Reagan, I believe that at this stage the relationship of strategic power between the United States and the Soviet Union can best be defined by the somewhat cumbersome phrase "strategically ambiguous equivalence." In using this phrase, I intend to convey the thought that at this stage neither side can be even the least bit confident about the outcome of a surprise attack/second strike response by either side or of a military conflict that escalates to a nuclear exchange on the basis of a protracted crisis permitting both sides to fully generate their forces. There is simply no rational way to anticipate confidently the likely consequences of either scenario, given the uncertainties regarding the actual performance in battlefield circumstances of existing arsenals, not to speak of the reliability of existing command, control, and communications facilities or of the likely behavior of the respective political leaderships under maximum psychological stress.

The merit of the volume lies in the systematic linkage between the development of the Soviet nuclear strategy and the political context in which it has matured. Soviet global political expansionism is highly dependent on that linkage, which exploits strategic parity (or strategically ambiguous equivalence) to pursue a politically assertive policy while avoiding a head-on confrontation. The authors base themselves on a solid grasp of the historical background, which helps to clarify for the reader the concept of political victory as understood by the Soviets. That concept is badly understood by the U.S. side, which in a mechanical way has concluded that existing nuclear parity has made the concept of political victory irrelevant.

The authors also help us understand more clearly how the Soviets assess the impact of the new reality of U.S.-Soviet strategic parity on U.S. behavior. This is an issue much underestimated in the United States. We simply have not taken into account the centrality, for the Soviet side, of the "liberation" of the Soviet Union from a setting of strategic inferiority. Even to this date, leading U.S. decision makers argue, with totally misplaced confidence, that U.S. strategic superiority was *not* relevant to the outcome of the Cuban missile crisis of 1962. The reason they do so is that strategic superiority was not central to U.S. calculations, which were based largely on the application of force derived from local-tactical superiority. What U.S. decision makers overlooked is the fact that on the Soviet side the existence of U.S. strategic superiority was absolutely central. The Soviet leaders knew that in a nuclear exchange at least 120–140 million Soviet citizens would perish, while the Soviet Union had the capacity at the time to kill approximately 20–30 million U.S. citizens.

To the U.S. side, such casualties were clearly prohibitive and they foreclosed the nuclear option insofar as the resolution of the Cuban crisis was concerned. What that analysis overlooked, however, was that the possibility of a nuclear war with the United States was much more horrendous to the Soviet side, foreclosing even those tactical counter-options where the Soviet Union enjoyed conventional superiority. To put it very simply, the Soviets could not respond to the U.S. naval blockade of Cuba with a ground blockade of Berlin, out of fear that such countermoves would lead upward on the escalatory ladder.

Today, though strategic parity has created an altogether different setting, the Soviet side continues to entertain the highest admiration for U.S. technological capability. This acts as a major source of restraint in the Soviet strategic calculations. The authors, in their study, demonstrate that this consideration plays a major role in the Soviet evaluation of "the correlation of forces." They do warn us, however, that "there is a real danger that technological competition will become so intense that the effort to define parity through arms control agreements will collapse. An open-ended and dangerously unregulated arms race might well be unleashed"—a warning that gives their book not only great analytical salience but direct policy relevance.

Zbigniew Brzezinski

Preface

The idea for this book came from discussions each of us had with two leading Western journalists, namely, the late Marc Gilbert of the Institut Français des Relations Internationales and Murray Marder of the *Washington Post*. Although the specific details of the discussions were different, the underlying theme in both cases was the need in the West for a nonpolemical book that attempts to lay out Moscow's views on strategic weapons and the implications that recent developments in the strategic arms race are having for Soviet military and foreign policy. This book represents a modest effort to fill this gap and is dedicated to Murray Marder and the late Marc Gilbert in recognition of the many hours of stimulating conversation we have spent with them. The loss of Marc Gilbert is deeply felt, and we note our appreciation of the continued friendship and love of Marc's family—Laurence, Jeremy, and Alexandre.

Although we wrote the book and take full responsibility for its content, its overall value was greatly enhanced by a number of our colleagues who provided their sage advice at critical points. First, and foremost, we thank Dr. Zbigniew Brzezinski for the kind words he wrote in the foreword. In addition, helpful comments were provided by the following persons: Raymond Garthoff, Rose Gottemoeller, Erik Hoffmann, Michael Mandelbaum, Richard Pipes, Walter Slocombe, and Alexander Vershbow. The careful copyediting by Lisa Berland at Westview Press is appreciated. We also thank our wives and children, whose unfailing support and understanding has been more important than they will ever know.

Finally, we wish to underscore the difficulties confronting the analyst of Soviet strategic arms policy. The key to a comprehensive analysis of the Soviet strategic challenge is to combine both political and military dimensions; too often the two dimensions are isolated from one another. In addition, Soviet sources are often opaque in meaning. Furthermore, Western analysts are too often engaged in ideological infighting, rather than a search for truth.

To develop as accurate a picture of Soviet strategic arms policy as possible, we have drawn upon a broad variety of sources. In the first chapter, our analysis of the evolution of Soviet policy draws upon Western sources as well as the most authoritative statements of Soviet military and political leaders. This chapter represents our best effort to distill the essence of Soviet doctrine as it has evolved over time.

In the second chapter, we have used Western data about Soviet and U.S. strategic weapons. We use these data to make "rational man" judgments concerning the "objective" implications for the Soviet Union of fighting an all-out nuclear war. By rational man judgments, we mean judgments concerning Soviet capabilities to conduct nuclear war implicit in their strategic force posture. In the previous chapter, we reached the conclusion that Soviet leaders have accepted such judgments. In the second chapter, we simply present the data that would confirm the legitimacy of such a conclusion.

In the third chapter, we provide our interpretation of how the Soviets might fight a nuclear war. Two types of sources are used. First, we have drawn upon the most authoritative Soviet military writings dealing with operational considerations. Most frequently, we have used materials published in *Voennaia Mysl'*, the classified Soviet General Staff journal, which has been declassified through 1973. Second, we make "rational man" judgments about Soviet options for the conduct of nuclear war based on the Soviet force structure.

In the fourth chapter, we interpret how Soviet analysts have characterized the evolution of U.S. strategic policy. We have done so in order to provide an interpretation of how the Soviets view the U.S. military-technological threat. The major sources of information for this chapter have been the published materials of analysts who work for Soviet foreign policy institutes, notably, the USA Institute and the Institute of the World Economy and International Relations. For a more extensive treatment of Soviet perceptions of the U.S. technological challenge, the reader is referred to Erik Hoffmann and Robbin Laird, *The "Scientific-Technological Revolution" and Soviet Foreign Policy* (Elmsford, New York: Pergamon Press, 1982), Chapter 4.

In the fifth chapter, we analyze the Soviet concept of strategic parity as revealed by Soviet arms control behavior, drawing extensively upon the writings and experiences of U.S. arms control negotiators in the strategic arms limitation talks of the 1970s. We also furnish an interpretation of Soviet behavior in the intermediate range nuclear force talks, but here we must rely on published Soviet and Western materials issued in the midst of the Western-Soviet struggle over this difficult and ongoing issue.

In short, we draw upon as broad a variety of sources as possible to provide as accurate a picture as possible of Soviet strategic arms policy. We recognize that such an effort is limited by the incompleteness of data and the polemical quality of much of the debate. We hope simply that our stab at a comprehensive and objective analysis is worthy of dedication to our friends Marc Gilbert and Murray Marder.

Robbin F. Laird
Dale R. Herspring

Introduction

This book is designed to provide a general overview of the Soviet strategic arms effort, especially since the onset of U.S.-Soviet strategic parity in the early 1970s. In fact, an alternative title for the book might have been "The Soviet Union and Nuclear Weapons in the Age of Strategic Parity." Although the first chapter deals with the superpower force structures that make up the contemporary strategic balance, the major thrust of the book addresses the problem of characterizing the meaning and significance of the Soviet nuclear challenge to the West.

Characterizing the Soviet strategic challenge calls for answers to four central questions. First, do Soviet leaders believe in the reality of mutual deterrence? For the United States, the reality of mutual assured destruction (MAD) has historically formed the basis of strategic doctrine. MAD, as a doctrine, aims at persuading the enemy that the costs of a nuclear war (in terms of losses) far outweigh any possible gains.[1] MAD places primary emphasis on the need for both the United States and the Soviet Union to maintain mutual vulnerability. By this, the United States has meant the ability of each side to deliver a vigorous second strike that would inflict "unacceptable damage" on the side that initiated a first strike. As a consequence of this view, the United States believes that both sides are thereby dissuaded from beginning a nuclear war. Do Soviet leaders also believe in such dissuasion?

Second, do the Soviets believe they could survive and win a strategic nuclear war? This question can be posed in two other ways. Do the Soviets believe nuclear war is a rational instrument for achieving political ends? Has the Kremlin adopted a war-fighting doctrine that it believes can enable it to win a nuclear conflict?

Third, do the Soviets accept strategic parity with the United States as a desirable, even inevitable, state of affairs or merely as a transient one? Specifically, do the Soviets believe that strategic parity exists? If so, are they prepared to accept such a condition over the long run?

Most importantly, do they believe strategic superiority is possible in the light of U.S. capabilities and are they working toward achieving it?

Fourth, does the Soviet approach to arms control embody a concept of strategic parity? Are the Soviet leaders seriously interested in limiting strategic arms or are they using arms control negotiations only as a vehicle for controlling—or defusing—Western efforts to meet the Soviet strategic challenge?

The characterization of the Soviet strategic arms effort has been a highly controversial process in the West. Some argue that the USSR primarily sees its strategic weapons as a deterrent to protect the Soviet Union from U.S. attack. The Soviets are in the strategic arms race to ensure that the United States does not gain a usable strategic superiority. From this point of view, the Soviets are interested primarily in strategic stability and parity, not in engaging in an unbridled arms race.

Others argue that the Soviet Union intends to achieve usable strategic superiority to advance its policy interests. Indeed, the strategic arms race is seen as caused primarily by the Soviet desire to establish global dominance by means of strategic superiority. The Soviets seek military superiority by winning the strategic arms race.

These two polar positions have entailed quite different responses to the four key questions identified in this introduction. To further elaborate these conflicting positions as well as to further analyze the nature of the four key questions, the views of Raymond Garthoff, a former member of the U.S. delegation to the Strategic Arms Limitation Talks (SALT), are compared with those of Richard Pipes, a former member of the National Security Council in the Reagan administration.

For Raymond Garthoff, mutual assured destruction is the basis not only of U.S. policy but of Soviet strategic policy as well.[2] As he sees it, the Soviet political and military leadership recognize that "under contemporary conditions there is a strategic balance between the two superpowers which provides mutual deterrence; that the nuclear strategic balance is basically stable, but requires continuing military efforts to assure its stability and continuation."[3] As a consequence, Garthoff sees Soviet efforts in the strategic area as aimed primarily at maintaining a mutual deterrent capability, not at gaining strategic superiority. Furthermore, he maintains, the Soviet leadership recognizes that the strategic balance is unlikely to shift significantly in the foreseeable future away from the reality of mutual assured destruction.

Garthoff then goes on to argue that "it is not accurate, as some Western commentators have done, to counterpose Soviet military interest in a warfighting and warwinning capability to a deterrent capability."[4] To the degree such capabilities are present, they are aimed at providing Moscow with "the most credible deterrent,"[5] in addition to serving as "a contingent resort if war should nonetheless come."[6] In practice, Garthoff would maintain, this means assuring that Moscow possesses the ability to deliver a credible and devastating retaliatory strike if that becomes necessary. Soviet nuclear weapons deployments do not imply a belief in the viability of nuclear war as a rational instrument of policy. Soviet leaders recognize that a nuclear war would be mutual suicide in terms of casualties and the amount of damage both sides would suffer. If, however, nuclear war should occur, Moscow's goal would be "to emerge from it victorious, that is, less totally destroyed than 'capitalism'."[7]

For Garthoff, the Soviets have accepted the existence of strategic parity since the early 1970s. This includes the Soviet military, which he maintains has acknowledged "throughout the 1970s . . . that while each side has certain areas of superiority, these balance out to yield an overall parity."[8] It is this parity that serves as the basis for Moscow's acceptance of the doctrine of mutual deterrence in Garthoff's view.

Despite their acceptance of parity, Soviet leaders continue to "display considerable suspicion of American intentions and concern over growing American capabilities."[9] The Soviets believe that the United States is engaging in an effort to obtain military "superiority." Moscow believes it must keep pace with the technological competition with the United States if it hopes to ensure that the Soviet nuclear deterrent remains credible. From this standpoint, Moscow's continuing strategic arms modernization program is explained by the technological competition with the United States.

Moscow's interest in strategic arms control negotiations is closely tied to its desire to maintain overall strategic parity. As Garthoff puts it: "The Soviet political and military leadership has recognized . . . that agreed strategic arms limitation can make a contribution, possibly a significant one, to reducing . . . otherwise necessary reciprocal military efforts."[10] As an example, he cites Moscow's willingness to sign the Anti-Ballistic Missile (ABM) Treaty. Had the United States continued with its ABM program, there was concern in Moscow that it could have restored the United States "to a position of superiority that could imperil the still unstable state of mutual assured destruction and mutual deterrence."[11] Thus, for Moscow, strategic arms treaties are not a vehicle for obtaining strategic superiority but an instrument for maintaining the nuclear balance.

In contrast to Garthoff, Pipes maintains that the Soviets reject the very basis upon which the Western concept of mutual deterrence is based. They believe in the possibility of winning a nuclear war and totally reject the concept of mutual vulnerability. Insofar as the concept of stability is concerned, "Soviet strategists regard 'mutual deterrence' to be a reality of the balance of nuclear forces as presently constituted, but they mean to alter this balance in their favor and in this manner secure a monopoly on deterrence."[12]

Furthermore, Pipes does not believe the Soviets are about to intentionally leave their country vulnerable to a second strike by the United States. Such a way of thinking is totally foreign to the Russian psyche. In fact, rather than retaliation, it is offensive actions combined with appropriate defensive measures against a retaliatory strike that are the focal point of Moscow's strategic policy. Finally, instead of avoiding any actions that might be viewed as threatening by the other side, the Soviets will do whatever they can get away with to assure their own defense. If the United States wants to follow a strategy of mutual deterrence, so be it; the Soviet Union is not interested.

Moreover, Pipes argues that although Moscow would prefer to avoid a nuclear war if at all possible, "Soviet doctrine . . . emphatically asserts . . . that its outcome would not be mutual suicide: the country better prepared for it and in possession of superior strategy could win and emerge a viable society."[13] Although Pipes does not directly deal with the question of whether or not the Soviet Union believes it can effectively employ the threat of using nuclear weapons for political purposes (e.g., to force the United States to back down in a crisis situation somewhere in the Third World), his heavy reliance on the Clausewitzian dictum that war is nothing more than a continuation of politics in another form at least opens the door for such an interpretation.

Pipes characterizes the Soviet strategic force posture as one which is counterforce in character. This means that Soviet strategic forces are primarily targeted at the enemy's military forces and especially the command and control facilities. The only purpose for such a doctrine, Pipes implies, is a desire to fight and win a nuclear war. In addition, unlike the United States, Moscow has devoted considerable effort to developing a defensive capability, most notably, air defense and civil defense programs. Such undertakings are clearly aimed, in Pipes's view, at developing a nuclear war-fighting, war-winning capability. Although the Soviets would prefer to avoid fighting a strategic nucelar war, they recognize that it may someday occur and if that happens, Moscow intends to be in a position to win.

Strategic parity may in some instances be a fact of life. If this is the case, Pipes would maintain, the Soviets do not accept it as a desirable condition. They do not want to give the United States the capability of deterring them. Given the heavy military input into the making of Soviet strategic arms policy, the Soviets probably believe that the only viable long-term option is the attainment of strategic superiority. Moscow's continuing strategic arms buildup is explained primarily by the drive for strategic superiority. In a word, Moscow is not interested in a "sufficiency in weapons, but superiority."[14]

Because Pipes characterizes the strategic balance between the United States and the USSR as inherently unstable due to Moscow's push for superiority, he seriously questions the value of strategic arms control agreements. Such agreements have in the past, he notes, focused mainly on "numbers of strategic weapons."[15] Qualitative improvements are equally important in his opinion. Most significant in Pipes's view, however, are Soviet intentions. After all, he maintains, "The Soviets persist in adhering to the Clausewitzian maxim on the function of war."[16] As a result, mutual deterrence on which both SALT I and SALT II were based is absent in Moscow's eyes. For Moscow, arms control negotiations are primarily aimed at limiting U.S. capabilities, especially constraining U.S. technology. Nevertheless, Pipes leaves open the possibility that arms control negotiations could be in the U.S. interest, but only if more account is taken of the serious differences between U.S. and Soviet doctrine and policy than has been done in the past.

The argument in this book will incorporate elements from both positions. We will argue that the "objective reality" of the U.S.-Soviet strategic balance is one in which both sides are currently capable of inflicting high levels of damage to each other with the delivery either of first or second strategic strikes.

Mutual Assured Destruction

We maintain that Soviet leaders, both civilian and military, recognize the objective reality of assured destruction in an all-out nuclear war. The acceptance of assured destruction has led to important modifications in Soviet military and diplomatic strategy. For example, given Soviet perception that the costs of a nuclear war outweigh any possible gains, we argue that the significance of conventional and theater nuclear forces for Soviet strategy has increased markedly. Furthermore, not only have conventional and theater systems become more important in the military dimension, they are also playing an ever more important role in Moscow's diplomatic strategy. The Soviet leaders believe that the more stable the deterrent to escalation provided by the strategic nuclear balance, the more effective conventional military advantage becomes as a diplomatic currency. Conventional military power is an especially critical tool in expanding Soviet influence in the Third

World. Without a secure strategic balance, the use of conventional forces in the Third World would create greater risks of unacceptable escalation.

War-fighting Strategy

The extensive and massive destruction that would result from an all-out strategic nuclear exchange has led the Soviets to reshape their military thinking. Soviet military writers have shifted the focus of their attention away from preparing to fight an all-out nuclear war against the West as the key military option. Rather, they have emphasized the creation of more flexible military options. Soviet military theorists and officials seek to create escalation dominance whereby the Soviets might prevail in a war with the United States without the fearful necessity of using strategic weapons. If the Soviets are developing a war-winning strategy, it is one founded on terminating a war in Europe without the need to risk significant strategic exchanges with the United States, because the United States would be deterred from using nuclear weapons by Soviet strategic nuclear power.

Strategic Parity

The Soviet approach to developing a military doctrine and force structure designed to win a war against the West is rooted in strategic deterrence that increases the military efficacy of military forces below the strategic nuclear threshold. It does not require the attainment of decisive Soviet strategic nuclear superiority. Strategic parity is thus a tolerable condition from a Soviet standpoint.

From a diplomatic standpoint, strategic parity with the United States, rather than superiority, is all that is required for the expansion of Soviet global influence. The loss of U.S. strategic superiority has been an integral part of the dispersion of global power, a process the Soviets hope to turn to their advantage. For Soviet analysts, the loss of U.S. strategic superioritiy is a critical component in gaining U.S. recognition of the Soviet Union as a power equal to itself. Soviet leaders also believe that strategic parity increases U.S.–West European tensions which they hope to exploit and thereby weaken the Western alliance.

Strategic parity has an inherent instability in the Soviet view due to the technological competition with the United States. The Soviet Union, of course, holds the United States responsible for "causing" the technological arms race. Nonetheless, in spite of technological uncertainties, the Soviets believe strategic parity will continue to prevail given the will of the Soviets not to lose in the strategic arms race.

The Interaction Between Arms Control and Strategic Parity

The Soviets participated in the SALT talks in the 1970s and the Intermediate Nuclear Force (INF) and Strategic Arms Reduction Talks (START) in the 1980s to ensure that strategic parity remained within reach. The Soviets used these talks primarily to try to restrain U.S. technological virtuosity. The Soviets also participated in the talks in order to generate domestic pressure on Western governments from their publics to support parity, rather than superiority. In addition, Soviets participated in order to enhance the stability of the environment for their defense planning.

This book is organized around four major categories by which we characterize the Soviet strategic challenge, namely, mutual assured destruction, war-fighting strategy, strategic parity, and arms control. The first chapter provides an historical overview of the changing role of strategic nuclear weapons in Soviet military and foreign policy. The second chapter describes the Soviet strategic force structure, compares Soviet and U.S. forces, and evaluates the "objective reality" of assured destruction inherent in the contemporary strategic balance. The third chapter analyzes Soviet thinking about and force structure options for the conduct of nuclear war. The fourth chapter probes Soviet writings about U.S. military policy to determine indirectly Soviet judgments about strategic parity. The fifth chapter examines the Soviet concept of strategic parity evidenced in the Soviet negotiating behavior in the SALT talks of the 1970s and the INF talks of the 1980s with the United States.

Finally, the book concludes with an assessment of the impact of the Soviet Union on the future of the strategic arms race. Although there are plateaus in the U.S.-Soviet strategic competition that can be crystallized in the form of arms control agreements, there is no end in sight to the ongoing competition itself. Between the pessimism engendered by the realization that the U.S.-Soviet strategic arms race is highly competitive and the optimism engendered by the realization that the Soviets are not so irrational as to seek global dominance through global nuclear war, the West must steer its course. It is not an easy task.

Notes

1. See, for example, Fritz Ermarth, "Contrasts in American and Soviet Strategic Thought," and Stanley Sienkiewitz, "Soviet Nuclear Doctrine and the Prospects for Strategic Arms Control," both in Derek Leebaert, ed., *Soviet Military Thinking* (London: George Allen and Unwin, 1981), pp. 50–69 and 73–91, respectively. See also Robert P. Berman and John C. Baker, *Soviet Strategic Forces* (Washington, D.C.: Brookings Institution, 1982), p. 33; and Keith B. Payne, *Nuclear Deterrence in U.S.-Soviet Relations* (Boulder, Colorado: Westview Press, 1982), pp. 11–27.

2. Garthoff's views are taken from Raymond L. Garthoff, "Mutual Deterrence and Strategic Arms Limitation in Soviet Policy," *Strategic Review* (Fall 1982), pp. 36–51 and pp. 58–63. Pipes's views are taken from Richard Pipes, *U.S.-Soviet Relations in the Era of Détente* (Boulder, Colorado: Westview Press, 1981), pp. 135–170, and Richard Pipes, "Soviet Strategic Doctrine: Another View," *Strategic Review* (Fall 1982), pp. 52–57.

3. Garthoff, "Mutual Deterrence," p. 37.

4. Ibid., p. 42.

5. Ibid.

6. Ibid.

7. Ibid., p. 44.

8. Ibid., p. 45.

9. Ibid.

10. Ibid., p. 37.

11. Ibid., p. 44.

12. Pipes, "Soviet Strategic Doctrine," p. 56.

13. Pipes, *U.S.-Soviet Relations in the Era of Détente*, p. 136.

14. Ibid., p. 159.

15. Ibid., p. 168.

16. Ibid.

1
Strategic Weapons in Soviet Military Policy

The role of nuclear weapons in Soviet military policy has changed over time. In the first phase (1946–1953), the Soviets denigrated the significance of nuclear weapons. The conventional superiority of the Soviet Armed Forces would be the key to victory in a future world war. In the second phase (1953–1956), the Soviets roundly rejected the conclusions reached in the Stalin period. Nuclear weapons had ushered in a "revolution in military affairs." The Soviets were trying to go nuclear as quickly and as broadly as possible. In the third phase (1956–1964), the Soviets placed their defense posture on the foundation of nuclear weapons and especially on the hopes for the rapid deployment of strategic missiles. In 1959, Khrushchev created a new service, the Strategic Rocket Forces, which immediately became identified as the premier element of the Soviet Armed Forces. Conventional forces were placed in a clearly subordinate role. In the fourth phase (1965–1971), the Soviets strengthened both strategic and conventional forces in order to implement adequately an all-out nuclear war-fighting option. Conventional forces became significant again, but primarily as a force to exploit the successes of strategic strikes in a world war. In the fifth phase (1971–1984), the Soviets recognized that assured destruction of Soviet society would result from fighting an all-out nuclear war. Politically, the Soviets recognized parity. Militarily, the Soviets enhanced military power below the strategic weapons threshold. Conventional military power regained a key position in Soviet thinking in its own right, not simply as an adjunct to the exploitation of strategic strikes. Conventional military power also was recognized as a key form of diplomatic currency, especially in expanding Soviet influence in the Third World.

The Primacy of Conventional Forces, 1945–1953

In the late 1940s and early 1950s, Stalin denigrated the importance of nuclear weapons and emphasized the relevance to modern warfare of the Soviet Union's wartime experience. The key to victory was in building a massive ground forces capability. Soviet strategy was built around the threat of occupying Western Europe with conventional forces in the event of war. Although the United States would be expected to retaliate with nuclear strikes against Soviet cities, these strikes would not defeat the Soviet Union, in Stalin's view. The United States would not be able to inflict unacceptable damage on the Soviet Union, let alone push Soviet forces out of an occupied Europe.

The successful Soviet strategy adopted during the conduct of operations in World War II was dogmatized by Stalin as the five "permanently operating factors" of war. Stalin declared that the following five factors would decide the "fate" of any modern conflict:

- the stability of the rear;
- the morale of the troops;
- the quality and quantity of divisions;
- the armaments of the army; and
- the organizational ability of the command personnel of the army.[1]

Once canonized by Stalin, the permanently operating factors could not be openly challenged. These factors became the centerpiece of Soviet military science and, in fact, dominated the field until after Stalin's death. The relegation of surprise to a secondary role, however, was to have a major impact on the development of Soviet strategic doctrine and the USSR's ability to react effectively to the introduction of nuclear weapons into the Soviet strategic arsenal.

Moscow's successes in World War II reinforced the Soviet commitment to the preeminence of ground forces. In fact, the Soviets appear to have counted on their massive conventional forces to counter the U.S. nuclear monopoly by holding Western Europe hostage to a Soviet invasion in the event of an attack on the USSR.

Despite the prominent role Stalin assigned to the permanently operating factors and to Soviet ground forces, he did not disregard the development of nuclear weapons. Indeed, he pushed Soviet programs aimed at acquiring nuclear weapons and deploying rockets.[2] By 1949, Moscow had exploded an atomic device and by 1953 a thermonuclear device. Efforts to improve Soviet defenses against the U.S. strategic threat were symbolized by the withdrawal of air defense forces from the command of the Soviet Army and their reorganization as an independent service—the Air Defense Forces. In terms of aircraft, Stalin showed a clear preference for fighters and ground support aircraft. Nevertheless, during the late 1940s, the Soviets began to deploy their first strategic system, the TU-4 Bull bomber which was a copy of the U.S. B-29. By 1953, about 1,500 were operational. According to one source, "these bombers could be used to counter regional threats from Western conventional forces or from forward-deployed, nuclear aircrafts of the United States."[3] Moscow was still, however, a long way from matching what it perceived as the U.S. nuclear threat.

Despite major technological changes, Soviet military doctrine continued to downplay the role of surprise. For example, in a highly authoritative article in 1950, General V. Kurasov reiterated the importance of the permanently operating factors, "which determined the fate of the war," while downplaying the role of "various favorable attendant circumstances."[4] As a result, Soviet military doctrine was becoming increasingly incompatible with the widespread introduction of nuclear weapons. The refusal to recognize the importance of surprise in a nuclear age seriously constrained Soviet efforts to make the major changes necessary to protect the country from a surprise attack. The net result was that while "Stalin moved the Soviet Union into the nuclear weapons age technologically . . . he promulgated a doctrine that viewed the new weapons as requiring no basic alteration in the political or military policy of the Soviet Union."[5]

Doctrinal Recognition of the Nuclear Factor, 1953–1955

In September 1953, only months after Stalin's death, an article was published in the official and authoritative Soviet General Staff journal, *Military Thought*, entitled "On the Question of the Character of the Laws of Military Science." Its author, Major General Nikolai A. Talenskii, questioned the validity of Stalin's permanently operating factors. "The thesis of the permanently operating factors by its very nature is not and cannot be a basic law of military science; it did not set as its goal the formulation of this law, not even to determine its actual content."[6] Talenskii also obliquely suggested that surprise could play a more important role than Stalin had assigned to it. He further called for a discussion in the pages of *Military Thought* on the subject. As a result of Talenskii's article, "The imprint of Stalin upon Soviet military thought . . . was being shaken."[7] Throughout the next two years a debate took place in the pages of *Military Thought* regarding the impact of nuclear weapons upon warfare. During the first eighteen months, the older strategic doctrine—the permanently operating factors—was attacked and somewhat modified, "but no official position was taken in favor of a revision of Soviet military doctrine."[8]

Nonetheless, because of the growing impact of nuclear weapons, the Soviets could no longer ignore the role of surprise in warfare.

The increased significance of the role of surprise was at the core of the argument in the single most important article to appear in the pages of *Military Thought* during the debate over the revision of Soviet strategy. The article was written by Marshal P. Rotmistrov and was published in March 1955.[9] The article had originally been rejected by the editors of the journal because of its implicit criticism of Stalin's permanently operating factors. While recognizing their importance for victory, Rotmistrov argued that surprise could have a decisive impact on the course and outcome of a war. The logical conclusion was that "since a simple effort to *repulse* an attempted enemy attack might be insufficient, a 'preemptive' or 'forestalling' strike was necessary."[10]

Following the appearance of the Rotmistrov article, other articles began to appear in which the role of surprise was acknowledged. Furthermore, the inadequacy of the old Stalinist formulation also came under increasing attack. The editors of *Military Thought,* for example, in the article that concluded the discussion of the Talenskii piece, made the following statement in reference to the permanently operating factors as the basis of Soviet military science:

> It is easy to see that in the best case this avoids a solution of the problem and is not a solution, and in the worst case it is a voluntary or involuntary withdrawal from the position of Marxist materialism. Indeed, this style of analysis can lead one unwittingly to conclude that there is neither "necessity" for a basic law of military science nor for another law, general and special, since in every general and particular case it will be permissible to substitute some factor or other for a law, saying each time the law is not important.[11]

In short, the Stalinist military strategy was being openly attacked because it led to "rigidity and complacency."[12]

Despite the increased significance assigned to surprise, it is important to stress that Soviet analysts were not arguing that surprise itself was a sufficient condition for victory. It might be a necessary condition for success under some conditions; it might have a devastating impact if used effectively. In practical terms, what Soviet theorists were saying was that if a war was imminent, it would be in Moscow's interest to launch a preemptive strike. As Stanley Sienkiewicz put it: "The Soviet solution . . . had to be premised upon the assertion that even were a surprise attack to be mounted, Soviet military power could still ensure victory. The obvious answer was to assert the capability to strike preemptively."[13]

Soviet military writers in the mid-1950s referred simply to the "possibility" of nuclear weapons being used in a future war, but that once nuclear weapons had been used such a war would "inevitably" become an all-out nuclear war. According to Major General G. Pokrovskii, "atomic and thermonuclear weapons at their present stage of development only supplement the firepower of the old forms of armament." Nuclear strikes could exert only a "significant" influence on the "course" of the war but could not exert a "decisive" influence. The decisive force in the war would be played by the ground forces. Such a war would inevitably become protracted in character, given the limited damage that rear areas would suffer, enabling them to continue to support the war effort.[14]

The debate over the impact of nuclear weapons spilled over into the political arena as well. In March 1954, for example, G. Malenkov, Stalin's immediate successor, stated that a new world war "would mean the end of world civilization."[15] This apparent acceptance of one of the main principles of mutual deterrence was opposed by Soviet military officials. They were concerned that Malenkov would attempt to use a deterrence strategy as a means for reducing military expenditure. This issue was one seized on by Khrushchev in his successful effort to oust Malenkov.[16]

By 1954, nuclear weapons had begun to be integrated into the Soviet Armed Forces. In the early 1950s, research and development work had begun on a series of tactical missiles, the SS-1 and SS-2, and by the mid-1950s an operational-tactical missile, the SS-3, was in the inventory of the Soviet ground forces.[17]

Changes in Western strategic forces in the mid-1950s had an important impact on Soviet strategic thinking. The Eisenhower administration had begun a worldwide buildup of nonnuclear forces and, most importantly, of tactical nuclear weapons in areas adjacent to the Soviet Union. This latter development, in particular, led to an increased emphasis on the Soviet Air Defense Forces. The USSR also took a number of further steps to counter what it perceived as an enhanced Western threat, including the upgrading of "its ground-based warning and control system, deploy[ing] surface to air missiles for the first time, and introduc[ing] high-speed interceptor aircraft capable of all-weather operations."[18] In addition, in an effort to threaten U.S. strategic forces, Long Range Aviation took on increased importance. The TU-16 Badger medium bomber, capable of delivering nuclear weapons, was deployed in 1954, and by the mid-1950s the first intercontinental bombers, the MYA-4 Bison and the TU-95 Bear, entered Moscow's inventory. The deployment of intercontinental ballistic missiles (ICBMs), however, was still several years away.

Soviet military analysts have characterized the mid-1950s as the period of the "revolution in military affairs." An authoritative Soviet history of the evolution of Soviet military doctrine identified the period as one which laid the foundations for contemporary Soviet strategic power.

> The essence of the revolution in military affairs is a sharp and profound transformation in the use of nuclear rockets as a means of struggle and of other corresponding means to achieve strategic goals in war. Combining nuclear weapons with rockets and automated control systems has led to the creation of new types of weapons—nuclear rocket weapons in which nuclear warheads are launched by intercontinental ballistic missiles. These weapons have changed previous ideas about the processes of preparing for the conduct of war, the roles and significance of time and space in these processes, the theaters of military activity, the correlation between types of weapons and types of wars, and the character of the interrelationships that are necessary to prepare for war.[19]

Nonetheless, it would not be until the Khrushchev and early Brezhnev periods that the promise of the "revolution in military affairs" would be realized.

The All-Out Nuclear War Option, 1956–1964

The Khrushchev period was characterized by innovation in many sectors of Soviet life, including the military sphere. Khrushchev both removed the inevitability of nuclear war from the Soviet ideological canon and enhanced the Soviet ability to wage it. In 1956, Khrushchev not only denounced Stalin, but the Stalinist concept of the inevitability of war with the West. The growing strength of the "socialist camp" meant that a nuclear war was no longer fatalistically inevitable. But such a war could be prevented only by being prepared to wage a nuclear war. The revolution in military affairs would have to be accelerated.

Khrushchev encouraged the process of rethinking strategy in military circles. Accordingly, in 1957 the Soviet Ministry of Defense convened a conference within the Soviet Armed Forces on military science and scientific research. The discussions were held in secret and closely followed by the party leadership. The conferees concluded that "the introduction of the nuclear weapon and the missile had brought about radical changes in all aspects of warfare, forcing major revisions in basic concepts."[20] The proceedings were published in *Military Thought* beginning in January 1960 and, according to one source, served as a guide for preparing Soviet forces to fight a nuclear war.[21]

The next major development in Soviet strategic doctrine came in a speech by Khrushchev to the Supreme Soviet on January 14, 1960. In this speech, which opened a new phase in Soviet military doctrine, Khrushchev declared that a future war would begin with missile attacks deep into the country's rear. He stated that while a surprise attack could be launched against the USSR, Moscow would be able to retaliate and would suffer less than the West due to the Soviet Union's size and dispersion of population. He also argued that nuclear wars would be of short duration. He argued as well that many traditional military forces should be replaced by nuclear weapons and missiles. Khrushchev then announced that Soviet forces (primarily ground forces) would be cut by one-third (from 3.6 million to 2.4 million men) and justified this planned reduction by claiming that increased firepower within the Soviet Armed Forces made them less dependent on large numbers of personnel.[22]

Khrushchev's doctrinal changes and cutbacks in force size were opposed by at least some segments of the Soviet military. For example, the Soviet military press, while avoiding openly critical comments, carried statements stressing "matters that Khrushchev had either glossed over or omitted altogether."[23] Furthermore, articles began appearing in the press stressing the problems that officers returning to civilian life were encountering.[24] In response to military pressure, the planned force reductions were cancelled in the summer of 1961 and the military budget was increased by 500 million rubles.[25]

Defense Minister Rodin Malinovskii's speech to the 22nd Congress of the Communist party of the Soviet Union (CPSU) in October 1961 marked another milestone in the evolution of Soviet strategic doctrine. In contrast to Khrushchev, Malinovskii reaffirmed the importance of traditional forces: "Final victory over the aggressor can be achieved only as a result of the joint actions of all the services of the armed forces."[26] In addition, he emphasized the need for "massive, multimillion armed forces" in order for the Soviet Union to be prepared for a protracted conflict, rather than a short war.[27]

A little more than a year after Malinovskii's speech, the first major work on Soviet strategic doctrine in over thirty-six years, entitled *Military Strategy*, was published under the editorship of Marshal V. D. Sokolovskii.[28] As might be expected, it maintained that nuclear weapons would play a key role in any future war. In accordance with Malinovskii's October 1961 speech, however, the book noted that conventional forces would play a major role in any conflict. It also underscored that the initial period of any war would be decisive. The book, however, contained a considerable amount of ambiguity in a number of key areas which almost certainly reflected continuing disagreements both between civilian and military leaders and within the military itself.[29]

A second edition of the Sokolovskii volume was published in June 1963. Although different from the first edition, it too left a number of important questions unanswered, including "the question of finding a strategy for victory in a possible future nuclear war where the usefulness of war itself as an instrument of policy is increasingly in doubt."[30] In addition, the second edition, like its predecessor, was beset with a basic ambivalence over whether victory could be achieved through a strategic nuclear attack or by a combined arms campaign. This suggested that differences within the political and military leadership over this question remained unresolved. Despite the absence of total agreement within the Soviet leadership at this time, however, doctrinal statements emphasized that a future war would be of short duration and would almost immediately escalate to involve intercontinental nuclear systems.[31] It was, as James McConnell of the Center for Naval Analyses put it, a period of emphasis on "all-out world nuclear war" as the basic Soviet war-fighting option.[32]

In 1957, the Soviet Union shocked the world when it launched the Sputnik into orbit using an SS-6 missile. The appearance of such a missile suggested that the Soviet Union would soon have the wherewithal to threaten the continental United States. Khrushchev seized on this development as the basis for the new Soviet strategy he announced in his January 1960 speech.

From a military organizational standpoint, the most important change introduced by Khrushchev was the creation of the Strategic Rocket Forces (SRF) in 1959. They were declared to be the preeminent service, a position formerly occupied by the ground forces.

According to Marshal K. Moskalenko, the first commander of the SRF, the strategic forces of the Soviet Union could exert a "substantial" influence on both the course and outcome of the war. The initial nuclear strikes would permit the attainment of the war's "immediate" objectives. The "initial period" of the war would be decisive in determining the entire "course and outcome of the war." Moskalenko also viewed the most likely kind of war with the West to be of "brief duration," a war that would, at most, last a few weeks.[33]

Despite the orbital launch of Sputnik, and Khrushchev's grandiose claims for Soviet missile capabilities, the fact of the matter was that the USSR was strategically inferior to the United States. For example, the missile deployed in the late 1950s and early 1960s, while useful in a theater mode, had no relevance as an intercontinental system. Furthermore, even when the first ICBM, the SS-6, was deployed, it was clear to the Soviet leadership that it was vastly inferior to the U.S. Minuteman. In a nutshell, Moscow was still not in a position to meet what it perceived as the U.S. threat.

Khrushchev adopted a threefold strategy to deal with the U.S. "threat." First, he emphasized the deployment of large numbers of increasingly sophisticated long-range missiles, as well as augmenting Soviet air defense. Second, the USSR began to show interest in arms control negotiations not only for propaganda purposes but as a vehicle for retarding U.S. weapons programs. Thus, despite Khrushchev's heavy use of arms control for propaganda purposes, he signed the Limited Test Ban Treaty of 1963. Third, Khrushchev attempted to rectify the strategic balance over the short term by placing medium-range tactical missiles in Cuba in the fall of 1962. His view of deterrence was based on a secure retaliatory capability, and he probably hoped to undercut his military critics at home by establishing a credible theater deterrent while effective long-range systems were being developed.[34] The failure of the plan was one of a number of factors that led to his ouster in 1964.

The Khrushchev period was a time of major change in Soviet strategic doctrine and force restructuring. According to William Hyland, editor of *Foreign Affairs:* "In the 50s and 60s strategic analysis was a new frontier; new ideas and thoughts were given relatively free rein; the Soviet Union was rebuilding its armed forces and thinking about the unthinkable. Extensive arming with nuclear weapons required the reexamination of military theories."[35]

Nonetheless, Soviet strategic doctrine was far in advance of available technology. To put it bluntly, Moscow's strategic forces were not up to the task assigned them, a fact that was made clear to the Soviet leadership not only by the Cuban incident, but by the Berlin crisis, the sharp deterioration of relations with China, and the adoption of a flexible response strategy by NATO. Nevertheless, the foundation for a massive buildup in strategic weapons had been laid, but it wasn't until the Brezhnev period that the strategic systems called for in Soviet doctrine began to enter Moscow's weapons inventory in substantial numbers.

Strengthening the All-Out Nuclear War Option, 1965–1971

The basic image of war for which the Soviet Union was to prepare was a more protracted but still an all-out nuclear war. Nonetheless, Soviet analysts began to underscore the importance of conventional forces in effectively implementing the all-out nuclear war option. The

Soviet leaders began to focus on a protracted phase of conventional war, especially as part of an occupation operation.

One of the most authoritative statements of the Soviet position in this period was by Major General V. Zemskov, the editor-in-chief of *Military Thought.* According to Zemskov, "in a nuclear war, if one breaks out, the combatants will use from the very beginning all the available forces and means at their disposal, above all strategic nuclear means." Nonetheless, there can be two periods or phases in such a war.[36]

The first phase would be characterized by the strategic strike. This would be a short period of intense destruction that would decrease the period of conflict overall. "In comparison with previous wars, a nuclear war, in regard to time, has the tendency of sharply decreasing its duration. This is explained by the vast material and moral loss which is inflicted during the first hours by the opposing states, as well as by the fact that in the course of it, both sides will be unable to replenish in a planned manner their armed forces due to the great losses in manpower and means of production."[37]

The second period would be characterized by protracted warfare. The military goal of this period would be to exploit effectively the results of the strategic strike. The remaining conventional capabilities of the combatants would be of decisive significance in the second period.

> Both sides, utilizing the surviving ground troops and forces of the navy and air force, will try to hold the initiative, realize more completely the results of the preceding nuclear strikes, and achieve the assigned missions. Both offensive and defensive operations of various scales are possible here. . . . In military operations in individual zones, as well as in theaters on the whole, lengthy operational intervals are not excluded. Active combat operations in particular regions might decrease and then break out anew.[38]

Zemskov's view of strategic warfare was one in which a protracted phase of conventional conflict would unfold after the necessary initial strategic strike has occurred.

Major changes were thus unfolding in Soviet strategic policy during the immediate post-Khrushchev period. As early as 1965, for example, General S. Shtemenko wrote an article that made allowance for the possibility of "non-nuclear warfare or of warfare restricted to tactical nuclear weapons."[39] In addition, Major General Lomov published an article arguing that "Soviet forces should be prepared not only for general nuclear war, but also for operations 'with conventional arms alone' or with 'limited employment of nuclear weapons.'"[40]

These new doctrinal formulations raised serious questions about Soviet doctrine as it had existed under Khrushchev. Wars could be *longer* than Khrushchev considered. The significance of general-purpose forces was thereby increased as the projected duration of the war increased. In essence, this meant that Soviet troops had to be prepared for a wide range of operations in the conditions of general nuclear war. To implement such a posture, general-purpose forces, which had been slighted during the Khrushchev period, would have to be strengthened in order to implement the all-out nuclear war option as it was now conceived. Increased concern with conventional forces, however, did not signify a lessening of Soviet concern over Moscow's ability to fight and survive an all-out nuclear conflict. Rather, the Soviet leaders conceived of a broader and more complex quality to an all-out nuclear war.

Great efforts were made during this period to build up Soviet strategic forces. The budget for research and development in strategic weapons was increased significantly.[41] Work was intensified on the development of an ABM system, a multiple independent reentry vehicle (MIRV), and newer missiles to cite only three cases. In addition, the number of ICBM launchers was also increased. For example, in October 1966 the USSR had deployed 340 ICBMs. A year later the number had risen to 720; by 1968 it stood at 900, and by 1969 it was 1,060.[42]

Furthermore, Soviet leaders continued to make qualitative improvements in their strategic systems. New types of missiles were deployed in dispersed and hardened silos. One of these missiles, the SS-9, was liquid fueled, carried a twenty-megaton warhead, had a range estimated at 6,500 nautical miles, and a throw-weight of 9,000–11,000 pounds.[43] In addition, the smaller liquid-fueled SS-11 with approximately a one-megaton warhead was also deployed.[44] Finally, the solid-fuel SS-13, which appears to have been intended "to serve as a strategic reserve for the Soviet land-based missile force" was introduced.[45] All of these missiles carried only one warhead at this time. Work was also undertaken to upgrade Soviet defenses against a U.S. attack. This included not only air defense forces, but command, control, and communications (C³) facilities as well.

The strategic role of the Soviet Navy also increased during this period. In 1968, for example, the Soviets introduced a new class of nuclear-powered submarine with sixteen tubes and equipped with the SS-N-6 Sawfly missile. Although the range of the SS-N-6 was 1,300 nautical miles at the time it was introduced, it was assigned "only a limited role in intercontinental strike missions against targets located in United States coastal areas, probably in part because its survivability in wartime is questionable."[46] Considerable effort was also devoted to increasing the navy's anti-submarine warfare capability, including the introduction of helicopter carriers. Finally, no new intercontinental bomber was developed during this period; the Soviet leaders continued to rely on the Bears and Badgers which had been deployed during the 1950s. The intermediate range Backfire bomber, however, was under development.

General purpose forces also received considerable attention. To cite only two examples, the navy's role was expanded to include the ability to operate away from home waters, and a naval presence was established in the Mediterranean. In addition, a new heavy transport, the AN-22, went into production in the fall of 1966.

Strategic Deterrence and Military Power, 1971–1984

As the Soviet Union achieved strategic parity with the United States in the early 1970s, the opportunity for bilateral negotiations to stabilize the strategic arms competition emerged. By signing the SALT I and II agreements in the 1970s, the Soviet leaders hoped to provide a more stable planning environment for their strategic modernization programs (to be discussed more fully in Chapter 5). The Soviet leaders also began to focus on the military implications of parity.

One such implication was the public recognition of the "objective reality" of assured destruction if a war with the West escalated to an all-out nuclear exchange. Brezhnev publicly committed himself to this position many times in the 1970s in settings targeted toward domestic as well as foreign audiences. Brezhnev referred to the ability of the strategic weapons of the superpowers to "destroy every living thing on earth several times." He also argued that in a general nuclear war "mankind might be wholly destroyed." He stated that a nuclear war would result in the "mass annihilation of peoples" and that "hundreds of millions" of people would die in such a war. He concluded in February 1981 at the 26th CPSU Congress that it would be "dangerous madness" for the Soviet Union and the United States "to count on victory in nuclear war."[47] Finally, in a speech delivered at a war memorial ceremony in Kiev Brezhnev stated: "It is a fact that the means of waging war, the means of mass annihilation have now acquired such a scope that their use would put into question the existence of many nations and, more than that, the whole of modern civilization."[48]

In light of the high probability of assured destruction resulting from fighting an all-out nuclear war, the Soviet leaders began to focus on strategic weapons as weapons to be used only if they had to do so. The professional military used this *political* realization to argue for the creation of a much broader array of military options below the all-out nuclear war threshold.

U.S.-Soviet strategic parity has increased the military and political significance of Soviet conventional and tactical nuclear forces within Europe. The Soviet Union under Brezhnev engaged in an impressive across-the-board modernization program of conventional forces in Europe. The conventional modernization program of the 1970s represented a reversal of Khrushchev's preference for strategic deterrence as the major force to guarantee the military balance in East-West relations.

The Soviet Union also engaged in an impressive nuclear modernization program in the European theater during the 1970s, but the impact of the development of Soviet theater nuclear forces on Soviet doctrine is ambiguous. On the one hand, at the rhetorical level, the Soviets have clearly denounced the concept of limited nuclear war, especially as enunciated by U.S. policymakers.[49] On the other hand, the Soviets seemed to have developed a force structure capable of being used to implement a Euro-strategic option, i.e., an option of fighting a nuclear war within Europe using tactical weapons without engaging in central systems exchange with the United States. As McConnell noted: "While, in its own eyes, Moscow has even yet not developed capabilities for tactical-nuclear and conventional warfare as *independent* options, there has been a gradual expansion of capabilities over the last 15 years on a dependent basis, to the extent that, with successive major pushes, there could be breakthroughs to independent options."[50] McConnell speculated that the USSR could have such a Euro-strategic option in the event of war by moving its Backfire bombers and other systems into Eastern Europe during a crisis, thus at least raising the possibility of a nuclear exchange in Europe occurring without a direct attack on the United States or the USSR.[51]

By increasing Soviet conventional and nuclear military capabilities in Europe in conditions of strategic deterrence, the Soviet leaders have increased the options available to them vis-à-vis the United States in a period of severe international tension. Deterrence in this case signifies the undesirability of crossing the threshold of fighting an all-out nuclear war. The stronger one's military power below that threshold, the more pressure one can bring to bear on one's adversary in a prewar or limited war.

Hence, Soviet recognition of strategic deterrence is coupled with an increase in the viability of its military options below that of all-out nuclear war. As McConnell noted, "Moscow has simply increased its *military* options and can more credibly pursue a greater range of *political* objectives; it is no longer restricted to those life-and-death issues that alone warrant general war."[52]

The political significance of the development of credible conventional and theater nuclear forces in Europe endows the Soviet Union with a sound basis for the exercise of influence in its relations with Western Europe. The effective deterrence of U.S. strategic power undercuts the credibility of the U.S. nuclear guarantee for Western Europe. A crisis of confidence is created within Western Europe and "interimperialist contradictions" are exacerbated. As Thomas Wolfe, formerly of the RAND Corporation, described this threat: "The preferred alternative from the Soviet viewpoint would probably be to see Western Europe eventually succumb to Soviet influence under a combination of enticements and pressures, helped in this direction by a growing sense of impotence in the face of preponderant Soviet military power."[53]

Nonetheless, military power within Europe only establishes preconditions for the exercise of Soviet influence. The successful pursuit of political power is not automatically ensured by any means. Hence, Soviet military power is conjoined with a détente policy in the attempt to exercise greater influence over Western Europe.[54] As one Soviet analyst described it, "The realists among the Western politicians understand that in this nuclear age it is essential to secure peaceful relations with the Soviet Union and other socialist countries, lessen the danger of a confrontation, and ensure peace and stability."[55] The goal of the Soviet effort is to attempt to ensure that an increasing concern will be manifest in Western Europe for Soviet interests and to encourage adjustments in Western European policy to those interests. Without a firm conventional and nuclear base within Europe in conditions of strategic parity it would be difficult to imagine how the Soviet Union would be playing as large a role as it is in the policy considerations of West European governments.

In addition, the occupation role that Soviet troops play in Eastern Europe and the political control they exercise increases Soviet influence over Western Europe by insuring Soviet dominance over the future of European security. Soviet forces in Eastern Europe also help to maintain order and serve as a bulwark in the unlikely event of a NATO–Warsaw Pact conflict.[56] But it might well be the desire to exercise political influence over Western Europe and thereby the United States that primarily accounts for the impressive modernization processes of Soviet conventional forces by the Brezhnev administration in the 1970s.

The Soviet preference for a combined arms approach is also evident in the Asian theater. The Soviets have built a large theater nuclear force to deter Chinese nuclear forces. But precisely because the Soviets believe that nuclear forces alone cannot deter military action on all levels, they have built impressive conventional forces along the Chinese border. This buildup has involved the deployment of over forty Soviet divisions which now constitute a virtually self-contained force, including major air and armored elements. The basic trend of the Brezhnev period has been to construct an increasingly independent military base in the Soviet Far East which is capable of sustaining military action against the Chinese and Japanese without involving Soviet forces in Europe or those that would become directly involved in a general war against the United States.

Outside of the Eurasian landmass, strategic deterrence has increased Moscow's ability and U.S. "imperialist" desire to exercise influence in the Third World through the direct use of the conventional military instrument in local wars. "Imperialism" has been "forced" by strategic deterrence to exercise its military power in various forms of armed violence below the nuclear threshold.[57] The most frequent target has been the Third World where "imperialism" recognizes that the most vigorous and open conflict between capitalism and socialism as world historical forces is occurring.[58]

Soviet analysts and policymakers have underscored the growing significance of Soviet military forces for power projection, especially naval forces, in the struggle between capitalism and socialism in the Third World. As an authoritative U.S. publication commented: "The Soviet leadership in the last two decades has awakened to the value of a powerful navy and other elements of sea power as tangible support for their nation's foreign economic, political and military policies."[59]

The Soviet use of its power projection forces reflects an acute sense of the political dimensions of the use of military power in the Third World.[60] Above all, the use of Cuban surrogates in a number of Soviet military interventions reflects a distinct Soviet preference to avoid direct conflict with the United States.[61] By avoiding direct conflict with the United States, the Soviet Union clearly isolates Third World military action from questions of general U.S.-Soviet military and especially nuclear confrontation.

The centrality of conventional arms to the realities of violence in the political development of the Third World means that military assistance has become a critical tool in the exercise of Soviet influence. Soviet Colonel E. Rybkin underscored this development as follows: "Oppressed and dependent nations waging wars of liberation were no longer alone in the struggle against colonizers. They received moral, political, economic, and, where possible and necessary, military assistance from countries of socialism."[62]

The growing significance the Soviets have attached to military assistance as an instrument of influence reinforces the importance of further developing Soviet power projection forces. Andrew J. Pierre in his study of the international politics of arms sales described the interrelationship between Soviet military assistance and power projection forces in the following manner:

> During the 1970s the Soviet Union greatly improved its capacity to transport arms over long distances by developing long-range cargo aircraft and by expanding its maritime capabilities. In the previous decade Moscow's ability to aid Lumumba in the Congolese civil war was limited. No such logistical problems hampered the impressive capability of the Soviet Union to bring Cubans to Angola and Ethiopia or to support them with sea and airlift operations, ferrying thousands of tons of arms and military supplies.[63]

Also, it appears that the Soviets have come to the conclusion that conventional arms in the Third World in both the forms of military assistance and Soviet power projection forces is the most efficacious way for the Soviet Union to compete with the West for influence in the Third World. Western economic power in the Third World is just too great for the Soviet Union to compete successfully on that basis, whereas on the military dimension the Soviet Union is in a much more favorable position to compete successfully.

In short, a condition of strategic parity between the superpowers has not reduced the perceived significance of military power to the Soviet Union. Rather, strategic deterrence has increased the significance of the effort to create usable military power, i.e., military power below the strategic threshold.

By creating more flexible military power, the Soviets are also more capable of fighting a protracted war with the West, even a war of significant conventional dimensions. In an authoritative statement on Soviet strategy, Marshal N. V. Ogarkov asserted the following:

> With the contemporary means of destruction, world nuclear war will [probably] be comparatively short. However, in view of the enormous potential military and economic resources of the coalitions of belligerent states, it cannot be excluded that it may also be prolonged in nature. Soviet military strategy proceeds from the view that if the Soviet Union is thrust into a nuclear war the Soviet people and their Armed Forces need to be prepared for the most severe and protracted trial.[64]

As of 1984, Soviet military doctrine, thus, emphasizes the significance of conventional forces in a general war scenario, but advocates flexibility in preparing for the use of nuclear weapons as well. As M. M. Kir'ian, a Soviet military analyst, put it, "A future war could be fought with both conventional and nuclear arms; beginning with conventional arms, it could at a definite stage become transformed into a nuclear war."[65] Similarly, an authoritative article in *Red Star* noted that "the present-day concepts of a non-nuclear war envisage linking the achievement of strategic results using conventional means with a readiness to repel a nuclear attack."[66]

The Soviet leaders envisage the possibility of a long conventional phase occurring before or after the delivery of insufficiently decisive nuclear strikes. Strategic reserves would thereby be called into play, either to be used in subsequent strikes against the adversary or for bargaining and war termination efforts.[67]

Soviet thinking about the increased significance of nonstrategic weapons is thus based in part on the question of the protracted nature of a future world war. It is based as well upon the more "rational" quality of conventional forces in meeting military and political objectives. For example, Fedor Burlatskii, head of the philosophy department of the Soviet Central Committee's Social Sciences Institute, underscored that fighting an all-out nuclear war would not be rational, for "there will be no victors in a nuclear war." But the irrationality of strategic warfare does not carry over into the conventional domain.

> Such is the dialectic of thermonuclear arms. . . . It is not at all like the logic of conventional arms, which remains as before; the army that is better armed is still stronger than the army that is worse armed, and in all circumstances the army remains the guarantee of a country's security. For an army with conventional arms is in fact in a position to defend its borders and its population. Conventional arms are instruments of security even in our day.[68]

Thus, for most Soviet analysts, the relationship between military power and politics in the nuclear age is a complex one. On the one hand, war—even global nuclear war—remains an essentially political act in which military power is used in an attempt to exercise dominance. On the other hand, the consequences of fighting such a war would be so devastating that the political rationality of fighting such a war is called into serious question.

Nonetheless, strategic deterrence becomes critical to ensure that military power can remain a rational instrument of policy. Effective escalation crisis management is critical to ensure that limited military actions do not lead to a general nuclear war in which means and ends become inverted. In such conditions, the significance of conventional arms as a practical instrument of policy increases.

Notes

1. For the text of Stalin's speech, see Iosif V. Stalin, "Order of the People's Commissar of Defense, February 23, 1945, No. 55," in Harriet Fast Scott and William F. Scott, eds., *The Soviet Art of War* (Boulder, Colorado: Westview Press, 1982), pp. 79–82.

2. William D. Jackson, "The Soviets and Strategic Arms," *Political Science Quarterly* (Summer 1979), p. 244.

3. Robert P. Berman and John C. Baker, *Soviet Strategic Forces* (Washington, D.C.: The Brookings Institution, 1982), p. 140.

4. Vladimir V. Kurasov, "On the Characteristic Features of Stalin's Military Art," in Scott and Scott, *The Soviet Art of War*, p. 85.

5. Jackson, "The Soviets and Strategic Arms," p. 245.

6. Nikolay A. Talenskii, "On the Question of the Character of the Laws of Military Science," in Scott and Scott, *The Soviet Art of War*, p. 128.

7. Ibid., p. 129.

8. Comment by the editors in Scott and Scott, *The Soviet Art of War*, p. 124.

9. The following material on the Rotmistrov article is taken from Raymond L. Garthoff, *Soviet Strategy in the Nuclear Age* (New York: Praeger Publishers, 1958), pp. 84–85.

10. Ibid., p. 85. Emphasis in the original.

11. Herbert S. Dinerstein, *War and the Soviet Union* (New York: Praeger Publishers, 1959), p. 51.

12. Ibid., p. 52.

13. Stanley Sienkiewicz, "Soviet Nuclear Doctrine and the Prospects for Strategic Arms Control," in Derek Leebaert, ed., *Soviet Military Thinking* (London: George Allen and Unwin, 1981), p. 79.

14. As quoted in Garthoff, *Soviet Strategy in the Nuclear Age*, pp. 78–79, 102–103, 108–113, 181.

15. As quoted in Garthoff, *Soviet Strategy in the Nuclear Age*, p. 23.

16. Ibid., pp. 23–24.

17. Berman and Baker, *Soviet Strategic Forces*, p. 41.

18. Ibid., p. 44.

19. *Sovetskie vooruzhennye sily: Istoriia stroitel'stva* (Moscow: Voenizdat, 1978), p. 412.

20. Harriet Fast Scott and William F. Scott, *The Armed Forces of the USSR* (Boulder, Colorado: Westview Press, 1979), p. 41.

21. Ibid.

22. For a partial text of the speech, see Nikita S. Khrushchev, "Disarmament for Durable Peace and Friendship," in Scott and Scott, *The Soviet Art of War*, pp. 162–164.

23. Thomas W. Wolfe, *Soviet Strategy at the Crossroads* (Cambridge, Massachusetts: Harvard University Press, 1964), p. 32.

24. Ibid.

25. Ibid., p. 141.

26. Rodin Malinovskii, "Address to the Twenty-Second Congress of the Communist Party of the Soviet Union," in Scott and Scott, *The Soviet Art of War*, p. 168.

27. Ibid., p. 169.

28. See V. D. Sokolovskii, *Soviet Military Strategy*, 3rd ed., edited with analysis and commentary by Harriet Fast Scott (New York: Crane, Russak and Co., 1975). The translation contains all three editions (1962, 1963, and 1968).

29. For a listing and discussion of these factors, see Wolfe, *Soviet Strategy at the Crossroads*, pp. 35–36.

30. Ibid., p. 52.

31. James McConnell, *The Interacting Evolution of Soviet and American Military Doctrines* (Alexandria, Virginia: Center for Naval Analyses, September 1980), p. 25.

32. Ibid., p. 2.

33. K. Moskalenko, "The Missile Troops Stand Guard Over the Security of the Motherland," *Krasnaia zvezda*, September 13, 1961.

34. Sienkiewicz, "Soviet Nuclear Doctrine," p. 75.

35. William G. Hyland, "The USSR and Nuclear War," in Barry Blechman, ed., *Rethinking the U.S. Strategic Posture* (Cambridge, Massachusetts: Ballinger, 1982), p. 60.

36. Major General V. Zemskov, "Characteristic Features of Modern Wars and Possible Methods of Conducting Them," *Voennaia Mysl'* 7 (1969), trans. in *Foreign Press Digest* (*FPD*), 0022-70, April 6, 1970, p. 19.

37. Ibid., p. 20.

38. Ibid., p. 21.

39. Thomas W. Wolfe, *Soviet Power and Europe, 1945–1970* (Baltimore: Johns Hopkins University Press, 1970), p. 451.

40. Ibid., p. 451.

41. For figures on published Soviet allocations for scientific research, see Wolfe, *Soviet Power and Europe, 1945–1970*, pp. 432ff.

42. Ibid., p. 432.

43. Berman and Baker, *Soviet Strategic Forces*, pp. 104–105.

44. Ibid.

45. Ibid., p. 54.

46. Ibid., p. 57.

47. All of the quotations from Brezhnev are taken from "Chernenko Rejects Use of Nuclear War to Achieve Policy Goals," *Trends in Communist Media*, Foreign Broadcast Information Service (FBIS), May 6, 1981, pp. 6–7.

48. L. Brezhnev, "Speech at Kiev War Memorial Ceremony," *Daily Report*, FBIS, May 11, 1981, p. R-5.

49. See, for example, Jack Snyder, *The Soviet Strategic Culture: Implications for Limited Nuclear Operations* (Santa Monica, California: Rand Corp., 1977).

50. James McConnell, *Interacting Evolution*, p. 92.

51. Ibid.

52. James McConnell, *Soviet and American Strategic Doctrines: One More Time* (Alexandria, Virginia: Center for Naval Analyses, 1980), pp. 34–35.

53. Thomas Wolfe in Richard Pipes, ed., *Soviet Strategy in Europe* (New York: Crane, Russak and Co., 1976), p. 161.

54. R. J. Vincent, *Military Power and Political Influence: The Soviet Union and Western Europe* (London: International Institute for Strategic Studies, 1975) (Adelphi Paper, no. 119).

55. *Western Europe Today* (Moscow: Progress, 1981), p. 382.

56. See Dale R. Herspring, "The Warsaw Pact at 25," *Problems of Communism* (September-October 1980), pp. 1–15.

57. For example, see Colonel E. Rybkin, "Armed Violence as a Form of Social Struggle and its Types," *Voennaia mysl'* 5 (1973), trans. in *FPD*, 0022-74, April 11, 1974.

58. See I. E. Shavrov, ed., *Lokal'nye voiny: Istoriia i sovremennost* (Moscow: Voenizdat, 1981).

59. U.S., Department of Navy, Office of the Chief of Naval Operations, *Understanding Soviet Naval Developments*, 4th ed., Washington, D.C., 1981, pp. 11–12.

60. See Stephen S. Kaplan, *Diplomacy of Power* (Washington, D.C.: Brookings Institution, 1981).

61. See, for example, Gavriel D. Ra'anan, *The Evolution of the Soviet Use of Surrogates in Military Relations with the Third World, with Particular Emphasis on Cuban Participation in Africa* (Santa Monica, California: Rand Corp., 1979).

62. E. Rybkin, "The 25th CPSU Congress and Wars of Liberation of the Contemporary Era," *Voenno-istoricheskii zhurnal* 11 (1978), trans. in *Joint Publications Research Service*, 072543, January 2, 1979, p. 42.

63. Andrew J. Pierre, *The Global Politics of Arms Sales* (Princeton, New Jersey: Princeton University Press, 1982), p. 77.

64. Marshal N. V. Ogarkov, "Strategiia voennaia," *Sovetskaia voennaia entsiklopediia* (Moscow: Voenizdat, 1978), vol. 7, p. 563.

65. M. M. Kir'ian, ed., *Voenno-tekhnicheskii progress i vooruzhennye sily SSSR* (Moscow: Voenizdat, 1982), p. 312.

66. *Krasnaia zvezda*, March 17, 1984, p. 2. This quotation was brought to the attention of the authors by Charles Petersen of the Center for Naval Analyses.

67. The material in this paragraph was provided in part by Rose Gottemoeller of Rand Corporation.

68. Fedor Burlatskii, "Novaia strategiia?" *Literaturnaia gazeta*, December 2, 1981, p. 14. This quotation was brought to the attention of the authors by James McConnell of the Center for Naval Analyses.

2
The Strategic Balance and Assured Destruction

To serve as a basis for our broader discussion of Moscow's perception of the role of strategic arms in the contemporary period, this chapter describes the Soviet and U.S. strategic force structures as of March 1984. Only deployed systems are discussed; systems under development are discussed in the conclusion.

In addition, the two force structures are compared and analyzed from the standpoint of the all-out nuclear option. It is argued from an objective standpoint that the U.S. strategic forces that oppose the Soviets have sufficient size (both in terms of launchers and in numbers of warheads), diversity (the "triad"), and survivability (especially with sea-based systems) to allow the United States to respond to even a Soviet massive first strike with a vigorous second strike. Such a second strike would be capable of delivering a devastating blow against the Soviet Union, especially against so-called countervalue targets, i.e., against cities and industrial complexes. But the Soviet force structure— especially if used in a preemptive strike against ICBMs—has the potential significantly to reduce the forces available to the United States for counterforce targets, i.e., the enemy's strategic nuclear forces including strategic C³ systems. Nonetheless, the significance of the discretionary force potential (i.e., strategic forces that remain after a preemptive strike) available to the United States is enough of a deterrent to the Soviets to make them wish to avoid all-out nuclear war.

The Soviet Strategic Force Posture

The Soviet strategic force posture is one that emphasizes centralized control over essentially a dyad of offensive forces—ICBMs and sub-marine-launched ballistic missiles (SLBMs)—with sufficient strategic defensive capability to permit centralized direction to continue throughout the duration of a strategic war.[1]

Soviet strategic forces would be under the policy direction of the Supreme High Command in wartime, an organization consisting of key members of the Politburo and the Ministry of Defense.[2] Operationally, these forces would be under the control of the General Staff which would coordinate the actions of the key services involved in strategic war fighting, namely the Strategic Rocket Forces, the navy, strategic aviation, and the PVO Strany or Air Defense Forces. The Soviet political and military leadership would place the highest priority on maintaining complete operational control over the strategic forces prior to, during, and following any type of strategic exchange with the United States, either limited or all-out.

Prior to a strategic exchange, the General Staff would rely on two basic types of systems to communicate operationally with its strategic forces.[3] The first type is a satellite communications system (SATCOM). The Soviets rely upon a low-altitude SATCOM system to provide their primary coverage from space. At least twenty-four of these relatively simple satellites are required to provide global coverage. In normal conditions, the Soviets maintain up to twice that number in orbit but in crisis situations the Soviets can be expected to launch more into orbit (eight are launched by one booster rocket). In addition to these low-altitude satellites, the Soviets can use two other higher altitude satellites to provide SATCOM links. One of these two can be used with mobile ground terminals providing the General Staff with more redundant SATCOM links.

The second and more numerous type of communications system is an extensive radio-based system which has both very high-frequency (VHF) and very low-frequency (VLF) capabilities. The radio-based systems which rely in part on buried underground cables provide the Soviets with a critical element of redundancy once strategic exchanges have begun. As is noted in a Carnegie Endowment Report, "Although the high-frequency radio systems are vulnerable to natural and nuclear atmospheric disturbance, they would provide a relatively inexpensive means of long-range communications, independent of satellites, after the atmospheric effects of a nuclear attack have subsided."[4] Because of the difficulty of easily restoring SATCOM linkages after a strategic exchange, the prior existence of the VHF and VLF radio links provides the most reliable postattack communications system between the General Staff and its strategic forces. The VLF systems are used primarily to communicate with Soviet submarines. The Soviets are currently developing an extremely low-frequency (ELF) communications system that will enable them to contact their strategic ballistic missile submarines (SSBNs) under a broader array of circumstances than is now possible.[5]

During a strategic exchange, the Supreme High Command and the General Staff would place primary emphasis upon the need to protect those political, economic, and military leaders responsible for the conduct of strategic war.[6] The Soviets rely in part upon a large network of hardened command posts or bunkers to protect the Soviet leadership. The Soviets have an extensive bunkered command system, the existence of which provides evidence of both the Soviet concern to ensure the continuity of centralized leadership and the recognition of the possibility of strategic war being protracted in character. *Soviet Military Power*, a Pentagon publication, noted:

> Soviet commanders and managers at all levels of the Party and government are provided hardened alternate command posts located well away from urban centers. This comprehensive and redundant system, composed of more than 1,500 hardened facilities with special communications, is patterned after similar capabilities afforded the Armed Forces. More than 175,000 key personnel throughout the system are believed to be equipped with such alternate facilities in addition to the many deep bunkers and blast shelters in Soviet cities.[7]

The quality or hardness of the command posts as well as their quantity are designed by the Soviets to provide for greater certainty of leadership continuity. They also greatly complicate U.S. targeting problems, because the United States would be required to expend a significant number of its strategic warheads in an effort to execute a massive strike against Soviet C^3 facilities, thus reducing the numbers of warheads for use against other Soviet targets.

The Soviets also rely upon mobility to protect the national leadership. The Soviets use several types of platforms to provide mobility, the most significant of which is the fleet of airborne command posts used by the General Staff and by the political leadership. The Soviets also rely upon ground mobile communications facilities, especially SATCOM and radio relay stations on wheels.

After suffering from the effects of either a massive all-out strike or from a limited strike in a protracted nuclear war, the Soviets would rely upon the mobility and redundancy of their communications systems and command posts and upon the hardness of their fixed sites to provide for the possibility of continued centralized direction of Soviet strategic forces. Such centralized direction is critical to determine the use of any remaining strategic forces, especially to coordinate their use with the remaining ground, sea, and air forces.

The Soviet leaders would be directing primarily a dyad of land-based and sea-based missiles of intercontinental range, relying only

TABLE 2.1
Soviet ICBMs

Type	Number Deployed	Warheads
SS-11		
Mod 1	100	1
Mods 2 & 3	420	1-3
SS-13	60	1
SS-17	150	4
SS-18	308	8-10
SS-19	360	6

Source: Based on data obtained from U.S. Department of Defense, Soviet Military Power (Washington, D.C.: Government Printing Office, 1984).

to a very limited extent upon the use of long-range bombers to deliver nuclear weapons against the United States. Based upon data published by the International Institute of Strategic Studies (IISS), we calculate that ICBMs, SLBMs, and bombers contribute 56 percent, 38 percent, and 6 percent respectively of Soviet strategic launchers, and roughly 70 percent, 20 percent, and less than 10 percent respectively of strategic warheads. This means that the dyad of ICBMs and SLBMs contribute more than 90 percent of the launchers and of the warheads for the Soviets. Within this dyad, the numbers of ICBMs are more than one and one-half times greater than SLBMs and carry at a minimum three times as many warheads as do the SLBMs. In other words, the ICBM component is the premier strategic strike force for the Soviets (see Table 2.1 for a summary of deployed Soviet ICBMs). SLBMs provide an important residual force and long-range bombers only a peripheral support role.

The most widely deployed and the oldest ICBM in service (since 1966) is the versatile SS-11. Currently, 520 SS-11s are deployed, in primarily a single warhead mode. The SS-11 was very widely deployed in the early 1970s, but since then over 500 SS-11 silos have been converted to house the SS-17 and SS-19 missiles. The SS-11 is currently deployed opposite the Soviet Union's borders with China, Europe, and the Middle East. The two silo fields to the east of the Carpathian Mountains house a mixture of SS-11 and SS-19 ICBMs, but the exact mixture of the two types is not known. The SS-11s would be able to cover all the key administrative and economic targets in the eastern and central United States and some of them have the range and qualities necessary to attack naval forces deployed at sea.[8]

The second most widely deployed ICBM is the SS-19 (360), a missile deployed with six warheads or a single warhead of high yield. The SS-19 carries the most accurate Soviet warhead. The SS-19 is designed to attack hard targets, especially U.S. silos, for which it is expected that a two warhead per silo coverage is required. This means that a single SS-19 which carries six warheads has the potential to attack three U.S. ICBM silos.

Almost as numerous as the SS-19, the Soviet SS-18 (308) is the largest deployed ICBM in either the U.S. or Soviet strategic arsenal. This "heavy" missile (so designated by the SALT agreements) has more than twice the throw-weight (ability to carry a payload) of the SS-19. The most numerously deployed versions of the SS-18s carry eight to ten warheads. Each SS-18 has the capability to attack four or five U.S. ICBM silos in a two warhead per silo attack. The initial deployment of the SS-18 carried a single large warhead of an estimated yield at least twenty-four times that of each of the multiple warhead versions. According to Robert P. Berman and John C. Baker, the large single warhead on the SS-18 could be used "for direct attacks against the United States national command authority and associated military commands or for sequential, high altitude, high megaton bursts in the patrol areas of United States launch-control aircraft and against the entire national communication grid. All of these targets are susceptible, to some degree, to the effects of electromagnetic pulses emanating from a nuclear detonation."[9]

The SS-18 is cold-launched rather than hot-launched like the SS-11 or the SS-19. The hot-launched technique requires engine ignition while the missile is in the silo with the silo becoming severely damaged from the launch. In contrast, the cold-launched technique involves a delay in main engine ignition until the missile has exited its hardened silo. According to the Pentagon report *Soviet Military Power,* "This technique minimizes launch damage to the silo and is consistent with the notion of building in the capability to reload and refire missiles during a protracted nuclear conflict."[10] This same report, however, cautioned that "the Soviets probably cannot refurbish and reload silo launchers in a period less than several days—thereby avoiding violation of the SALT II agreement which precludes a rapid reload capability for ICBM launchers."[11] Nevertheless, it is interesting to note that the Soviets in an exercise in the autumn of 1980 practiced the reloading of twenty-five to forty SS-18 silos during a period of two to five days.[12]

The Soviet ICBM force of SS-18s and SS-19s pose a grave threat to the U.S. ICBM force. As *Soviet Military Power* noted: "The force of SS-18 Mod 4s currently deployed has the capability to destroy more than 80 percent of the U.S. ICBM silo launchers using two nuclear warheads against each United States silo. The SS-19 Mod 3 has nearly identical capabilities."[13]

The next most widely deployed ICBM in the Soviet Union is the SS-17 (150), which together with the SS-19 is replacing the SS-11. The most important aspect of the deployment of both the SS-17 (four warheads) and SS-19 is the introduction of multiple warheads as compared to the SS-11. Both the SS-17 and the SS-19 also have improved accuracy, increased throw-weight, and greater survivability than the SS-11. The SS-17 is slightly longer than the SS-11 and is of larger volume. It utilizes the cold-launched technique, whereas the SS-19 relies upon the conventional hot-launched technique. The SS-17 has also been tested with a single large warhead having more than five times the yield of a single multiple warhead version. This warhead might be used against U.S. C³ facilities. The SS-17s have sufficient range and accuracy as well as high enough warhead yield to strike any U.S. ICBM base as well as Strategic Air Command (SAC) bases, and support facilities throughout the United States.

The final deployed Soviet ICBM is the SS-13. The sixty deployed SS-13s carry one warhead of medium yield with a relatively low level of accuracy. It is the only deployed Soviet ICBM that uses solid fuel as opposed to liquid fuel for its propulsion system. Solid fuels are marginally preferable to liquid fuels because solid fuel allows the missiles to be launched at the turn of a key. The Soviets rely upon storable liquid fuels for the majority of their strategic rocket propulsion systems. These missiles can be launched on short notice, somewhere on the order of four to eight minutes.

The SS-13 was deployed in the late 1970s and represented a shift away from large missiles in the Soviet inventory. The SS-13 was perceived by the United States to be the initial counter to the U.S. Minuteman but because of problems encountered with the last-stage rocket motor, the SS-13 has never been widely deployed. A direct follow-on to the SS-13 was the experimental SS-16 which has not been deployed, in part, because of technological problems and, in part, because of treaty agreements with the United States. Nonetheless, the first two stages of the SS-16 formed the rocket system for the widely deployed intermediate range ballistic missile (IRBM), the SS-20. Over one hundred of the SS-16s have allegedly been produced for testing purposes.

The SS-13s probably have a mission to attack "soft" military targets, such as army, naval, and air force bases in the United States. Berman and Baker hypothesized that "some of the SS-13s could act as a booster

TABLE 2.2
Main Soviet Nuclear Ballistic Missile Submarines and Missiles

Type of Submarine	Number Deployed	Type of Missile System	Number of Warheads per Missile
Yankee I	23	SS-N-6	1
Yankee II	1	SS-N-17	1
Delta I	18	SS-N-8	1
Delta II	4	SS-N-8	1
Delta III	14	SS-N-18	3-7
Typhoon	1	SS-N-20	6-9

Source: Based on data obtained from U.S. Department of Defense, Soviet Military Power (Washington, D.C.: Government Printing Office, 1984).

for emergency transmitters to relay communications while the majority of the SS-13 regiments attacked early warning systems in Canada and Greenland."[14]

The Soviets have deployed a substantial strategic reserve capability at sea to supplement their land-based ICBM force (see Table 2.2 for a summary of deployed SLBMs). The Soviets rely upon ballistic missile submarines to perform both regional and intercontinental strike missions. The three Hotel II and thirteen Golf II submarines carry a missile with a range limited to playing a theater role. It is believed that the additional Hotel III and Golf II (one each) submarines, even though deployed with a longer range missile, would play solely a regional role. This judgment is based on the limited operating range of the Golf and Hotel Class submarines.

The remaining sixty-one Yankee, Delta, and Typhoon Class submarines constitute the intercontinental strike force of the Soviet Navy. These SSBNs carry 920 submarine-launched ballistic missiles. The accuracy and yield of these warheads is such that the Soviet SLBM force could be used only against "soft" targets, i.e., nonhardened military targets, economic installations, and civilian populations. The range of the SLBMs is of two basic types; a medium range is carried by the Yankee Class SSBN and a longer range SLBM is carried by the Delta and will be carried by the Typhoon Class SSBNs. The range limitations of the Yankee Class require it to operate in the mid-Atlantic and mid-Pacific in order to be within striking distance of the United States. In contrast, the longer range SLBMs allow the Delta and Typhoon Class SSBNs to operate close to Soviet shores and yet remain within the range of U.S. targets.

Each Yankee Class submarine has sixteen vertical launching tubes arranged in two rows of eight. These twenty-four SSBNs carry 384 SS-N-6 missiles with a range of 3,000 kilometers. These missiles carry a single warhead of medium yield and of relatively low accuracy. The SS-N-6 has been tested with multiple warheads but appears not to have been deployed. The first Yankee was laid down in 1965 and delivered in late 1967 with the last of the class being completed in 1976. The original deployment of this class was to the eastern seaboard of the United States which provided coverage at least as far as the Mississippi. An increase in numbers allowed a Pacific patrol to be established off California which extended target coverage at least as far as the Rockies.

The target coverage of the SS-N-6s deployed on Yankees operating on patrol provides the Soviets with the potential for rapidly striking various U.S. command and control centers. As Berman and Baker noted, "One important target set within the American command-and-control system is the Strategic Air Command's airborne command aircraft. With their short flight time, the SS-N-6 SLBMs on the forward deployed Y-Class SSBNs could pose a significant threat to the small number of SAC bases housing the airborne command network, particularly those capable of launching and retargeting the Minuteman ICBMs."[15]

In addition, there is one twelve-tube Yankee II SSBN which is deployed as a test bed for the SS-N-17 SLBM. This is the first Soviet SLBM to use solid fuel and to be equipped with a postboost vehicle. The latter feature suggests a multiple-warhead capability although to date only single reentry vehicle payloads have been noted. It is possible that the SS-N-17 and its modified Yankee Class test bed were developed as the forerunners for the new Typhoon Class submarines and the SS-N-20 missiles.

There are two longer range SLBMs carried by the Delta Class submarines. Two-hundred and eighty SS-N-8s are carried by eighteen Delta Is and by four Delta IIs. The Delta II (sixteen launchers) differs from the Delta I (twelve launchers) primarily in its greater length which allows it to carry a larger number of launchers. The SS-N-8 which was first deployed in the early 1970s has three times the range of the SS-N-6. The range of the SS-N-8 allows the Delta Class submarine to reach its targets in the United States from safer home waters. In other respects the SS-N-8 does not represent a significant improvement over the SS-N-6. Both carry a single warhead and have similar yields and accuracies.

It was not until the deployment of the SS-N-18 on the Delta IIIs that increased payload was added to extended range. Each of the fourteen Delta IIIs carry sixteen SS-N-18s (224 SLBMs overall) which in turn are capable of carrying multiple warheads (three) of medium yield. The SS-N-18 has an improved accuracy over the SS-N-6 and SS-N-8s by at least a third. With the deployment of the Deltas, especially the Delta III, the Soviet SSBN force has come to share with the ICBM the deep strike mission against targets in the United States.

The latest addition to the Soviet sea-based strategic arsenal is the Typhoon Class SSBN. This submarine was launched in 1980 and is designed to carry the SS-N-20 SLBM. Larger than the SS-N-18, the SS-N-20 is powered by a solid-fuel propulsion system giving it a range of more than 8,000 kilometers. A payload of seven warheads is anticipated. The Typhoon displaces about 25,000 tons which makes it the largest SSBN in either the U.S. or Soviet fleets.

Soviet strategic submarines are deployed in three of the four main fleets of the Soviet Navy—the Northern, Pacific, and Baltic fleets. According to Berman and Baker, "About 70 percent of the submarines are assigned to the Northern fleet based at Murmansk on the Kola Peninsula; they are deployed to regular patrol areas in the Barents, Norwegian and Greenland seas, as well as forward to stations off the eastern coast of the United States. Most of the others are stationed with the Pacific Fleet at the submarine base at Petropavlovsk on the Kamchatka Peninsula."[16]

Finally, the Soviets rely only to a very small extent upon long-range bombers for the delivery of nuclear weapons against U.S. targets. The Soviets currently deploy 143 bombers with intercontinental strike range.

The Tu-95 Bear is a four-engine, swept wing, turboprop-powered bomber which is capable of delivering free-fall bombs or air-to-surface missiles. First deployed in the mid-1950s, about 100 Bears are still in service with strategic aviation. The Bear is able to carry a payload in excess of 25,000 pounds to a range greater than 11,000 kilometers. It is both the largest and longest range Soviet bomber. Six variants of the Bear have been produced, three of which have been for the strategic strike mission, two for reconnaissance, and one for anti-submarine warfare (ASW). Two of the strategic strike versions are designed to carry the AS-3 air-to-surface missile for a stand-off attack.

The MYA-4 Bison is a four-engine, swept wing, turbojet-powered bomber which is capable of carrying free-fall bombs. First deployed in the mid-1950s, about seventy are still in service. About forty of these are still operating as strategic bombers. The Bison is able to carry a payload in excess of 12,000 pounds to a range of about 8,000 kilometers.

Even a small number of long-range bombers are a useful supplement to the Soviet strategic strike forces. They provide some reserve protection through their mobility. Also, they can strike mobile targets such as aircraft carriers or SSBNs on patrol as well as U.S. early-warning radars located outside the continental United States. Long-range bombers also permit a follow-up striking capability to inflict further damage on U.S. targets inadequately destroyed by a Soviet first strike.

The Soviets are, however, in the process of beefing up their bomber force by making them cruise missile carriers. The cruise missile–bomber combination will substantially increase the importance of the bomber component of Soviet strategic forces, but the ICBM emphasis will remain.

In addition to their strategic offensive forces, which are summarized in Table 2.3, the Soviet leaders consider strategic defense a critical component of their war-fighting posture. The main goal of strategic defense would be to permit the central leadership to maintain control or direction over military forces and other defense assets, as well as to replace or reconstitute critical forces and defense assets throughout the duration of a nuclear war. Put in other terms, Soviet strategic defense is designed to protect the leadership, strategic offensive assets, and defense production assets in order thereby to provide the possibility for force reconstitution after either limited or all-out nuclear exchanges.

As discussed earlier, the Soviets rely upon a system of fixed and mobile command posts with an extensive communications network to enable the leadership to continue direction of the war effort. Unlike the U.S. system in which only the very top political and military leaders will be protected, the Soviets are striving to protect leadership throughout the whole country.

The protection of the key leaders in the Soviet Union is essential to war fighting from both a political and military perspective. From a political perspective, the hierarchic nature of Soviet society requires the maintenance of centralized control to ensure the continued functioning of the system. Key decisions tend to be pushed up to the top of bureaucratic organizations. Initiative by middle-level elites is discouraged. Habits of compliance by middle-level elites might well undercut their ability to make the kind of macro-level, systemwide decisions critical to national survival in a nuclear war. The high levels of destruction and disruption associated with strategic war would require an ability to husband critical resources and to apply them to those areas where they would have maximum effect. Thus, the con-

TABLE 2.3
Estimated Soviet Strategic Nuclear Warheads

System		Number Deployed	Warheads Per Launcher	Total Warheads
ICBM				
SS-11		520	1[b]	520
SS-13		60	1	60
SS-17	Mod 1	150	4	600
SS-18		308		2,500[c]
	Mod 1		1	
	Mod 2		8	
	Mod 3		1	
	Mod 4		10	
SS-19		360		1,710[d]
	Mod 2		1	
	Mod 3		6	
SLBM				
SS-N-5		57	1	57
SS-N-6	Mods 1&2	384	1	384
SS-N-8	Mods 1&2	280	1	280
SS-N-17		12	1	12
SS-N-18		224		1,120
	Mod 1		3	1,120
	Mod 3		7	
SS-N-20		20	6-9	160
Subtotal (ICBM and SLBM):				7,400
Aircraft				
Tu-95	100	2[a]	200	
Mya-4	43	2[a]	86	
TOTAL:				7,686

[a]Assumes two gravity bombs or air-to-surface missiles per aircraft.
[b]There are three Mods but Mod 1 has a single reentry vehicle (RV), and the three multiple reentry vehicles on Mod 3 are counted as one RV.
[c]Estimate based on the assumption that the bulk of SS-18 are Mod 2. While Mods 1 and 3 may carry a large single warhead, Mod 4 may carry ten RV.
[d]Assumes about 75 percent are Mod 3.

Source: Based on data obtained from The Military Balance, 1982-1983 (London: International Institute for Strategic Studies, 1982); The Military Balance, 1983-1984 (London: International Institute for Strategic Studies, 1983); U.S. Department of Defense, Soviet Military Power (Washington, D.C.: Government Printing Office, 1984).

tinuation of control by centralized elites is essential to the management of the Soviet war effort.

From a military perspective, centralized control is essential in order to ensure the continued ability of the Soviet Union to fight effectively, or possibly to fight at all. Desmond Ball, an Australian analyst, has underscored the significance to the Soviets of centralized direction and its uninterrupted control throughout a war in the following words:

> Observation of Soviet military exercises gives the impression that ships, aircraft, and commands have carefully and specially planned roles, and that operational communications flow directly between headquarters in Moscow and the individual units in the field. Local commanders seem to have relatively little scope to adapt general orders to field conditions or to use their own initiative if they do not receive central orders. This tendency could be even more pronounced in the strategic forces, since Soviet leaders would be particularly loath to allow lower commanders much room for initiative where nuclear weapons were concerned.[17]

The need to protect Soviet leaders and to ensure their continued ability to manage the system is thus central to any successful war-fighting effort. It is at the heart of Soviet strategic defense efforts. Such efforts are not only aimed at protecting the leadership but at ensuring the continued existence of military assets even in the face of U.S. nuclear attacks.

The Soviets rely on several types of military forces to provide protection for Soviet C^3 facilities and strategic offensive forces. The most important of these are forces for air defense and SSBN defense. Less significant due to the limited nature of their deployments and their capabilities are anti-ballistic missile and anti-satellite systems (ASAT).

Soviet air defense relies upon the use of interceptor aircraft in conjunction with early-warning networks and surface-to-air missiles (SAMs). There are more than 5,000 air defense radars throughout the USSR. The Air Defense Forces rely upon 2,500 interceptor aircraft, including the MiG-23 Flogger and the MiG-25 Foxbat. The Soviets are deploying MiGs (the MiG-29 and MiG-31) that, unlike the MiG-23, are capable of attacking low-altitude targets effectively. Finally, there are more than 10,000 SAM launchers which are deployed at more than 1,000 fixed sites.

The Soviet air defense system is charged with the task of defending against a U.S. bomber attack. Interceptor aircraft would be used to attack U.S. bombers before they penetrated Soviet airspace. Additional interceptor aircraft in conjunction with some SAMs would be available to attack aircraft that penetrated Soviet airspace. Finally, clusters of SAMs would be used for point defense of the target itself.

The major weakness historically of the Soviet air defense system has been the inability to defend effectively against a low-altitude bomber threat, precisely the kind of bomber force that the United States currently deploys. As Gordon Macdonald, Jack Ruina, and Mark Balaschak noted in a major study by the Brookings Institution:

> The currently deployed Soviet system seems to have been designed only for a high altitude bomber attack. Early warning radars cover all the important entry areas for bombers from the United States or Western Europe and can detect high-flying aircraft well beyond Soviet borders. Soviet interceptor aircraft and SAM batteries are numerous enough to inflict heavy attrition on any high-altitude attacking force. . . . For a low-altitude (500–600 feet) bomber attack the situation is substantially different. Although radar coverage in the northwest sector is dense enough to continue to provide some coverage, large gaps appear where radars are not densely distributed. The capability of Soviet strategic SAMs and current aircraft interceptors would be marginal at best against low-flying bombers. . . . The net effect is that a substantial fraction of the weapons carried in a large, well-planned, low-altitude bomber attack against the Soviet Union would probably be delivered to their targets. Highly defended point sites might inflict significant attrition on such an attacking force, but they would be unlikely to survive a heavy attack.[18]

Nonetheless, the Soviets with the addition of new SAM systems (the SA-10) and new air defense fighters (MiG-29 and MiG-31) are now deploying forces capable of threatening U.S. penetrating bombers flying at low altitude. *Soviet Military Power* noted that:

> Soviet air defenses . . . are in the initial stages of a major overhaul geared entirely to fielding an integrated air defense system much more capable of low-altitude operations. This overhaul includes the partial integration of strategic and tactical air defenses; the upgrading of early-warning and air surveillance capabilities; the deployment of more efficient data transmission systems; and the development and initial deployment of new aircraft, associated air-to-air missiles, surface-to-air missiles and an airborne warning and control system.[19]

In addition to air defense, the other most significant form of strategic defense is SSBN defense. The Soviets currently rely upon their SSBN force to provide them with a strategic reserve force. But in order for this strategic reserve to remain viable it must be protected against the significant U.S. and West European ASW assets. To maximize protection of their SSBNs, the Soviets operate bastions in the Norwegian and Barents seas in the Atlantic and in the Sea of Okhotsk in the Pacific. In other words, the Soviets are trying to turn a traditional geographic disadvantage—the absence of an open ocean seaport— into a critical asset for strategic defense. Ian Bellany described the Soviet effort in the following words:

> In order to reach open oceanic waters Soviet SSBNs emerging from either base (Polyarny near Murmansk in the West and Petropavlovsk in the East) first have to pass through one of two relatively narrow stretches of water. In the West it is the Greenland-Iceland-UK gap and in the East, the Aleutian-Japan gap. Both waterways have been "wired for sound" by the United States Navy using sound surveillance systems (SOSUS). And once the Soviet submarines are in oceanic waters, they enter an extremely hostile ASW environment composed of Western aircraft, surface vessels and hunter-killer submarines. For these reasons the Soviet Union started very early to look to ultra-long-range SLBMs as a way of salvaging her positions. This was not to give her SSBNs more sea to play in, but to allow boats to retreat from oceanic waters where ASW control is firmly in Western hands, towards shallower sanctuary waters closer to Soviet territory where Western ASW command of the sea can at least be disputed.[20]

To ensure the survivability of the SSBN force, the Soviet Navy has developed a strategic support mission in which its ASW forces are used to defend the SSBNs.[21] The Soviet Navy relies upon its land-based naval air force to track and attack enemy submarines. The Soviet Navy also relies on hunter-killer submarines to protect SSBNs. Finally, the Soviet Navy relies on its surface fleet to provide additional ASW capability. The Kiev Class aircraft carriers are useful in this ASW support role. Also useful in this role are the Kresta missile cruisers which carry ASW helicopters and anti-submarine cruise missiles. The Soviets also have built tunnels near their home ports to house and protect their SSBNs.[22]

In addition to SSBN defense, the Soviets maintain the world's only deployed system of ballistic missile defense. The system includes ballistic missile early-warning radars and four operational ABM launch complexes near Moscow which employ the Galosh interceptor missile. The Soviet Union is limited to an upper level of 100 ABM launchers by the 1972 ABM treaty, as amended in 1974. The USSR originally retained 64 Galosh launchers around Moscow but has removed 32 of them. According to *Soviet Military Power,* "the Soviets are upgrading this system to the 100 launchers permitted under the Treaty. When completed, the new system will be a two-layer defense composed of silo-based long-range modified Galosh interceptors designed to engage targets outside the atmosphere; silo-based high-acceleration interceptors designed to engage targets within the atmosphere; associated engagement and guidance radars; and a new large radar at Bushkino designed to control ABM engagements. The silo-based launchers may be reloadable."[23] In addition to the Galosh system, the Soviet Union has reportedly tested an advanced version of the SA-5 high-altitude SAM system against ballistic missile reentry vehicles as well.[24] The latest Soviet surface-to-air missiles (the SA-10 and SA-12) may also have the "potential to intercept some types of United States strategic ballistic missiles as well."[25]

The final system for active strategic defense is the ASAT system. The Soviets have deployed a nonnuclear low-altitude orbital ASAT interceptor. ASATs are launched by SS-9 missiles. *Soviet Military Power* described the Soviet ASAT system in the following terms:

> Using a radar sensor and a pellet-type warhead, the interceptor can attack a target in various orbits during its first two revolutions. An intercept during the first orbit would reduce the time available for a target satellite to take evasive action. The interceptor can reach targets orbiting at more than 5,000 kilometers, but is probably intended for high priority satellites at lower altitudes.[26]

U.S. reconnaissance, ocean surveillance, electronic intelligence, and navigational and meteorological satellites operate at altitudes under 600 miles. The space shuttle also operates in a low-altitude orbit. All of these low-altitude systems are within potential range of the current Soviet satellite interceptor. The Soviet ASAT, however, does not have any capability against U.S. early-warning satellites or against communications satellites that operate in higher altitude orbits.[27] Nonetheless, by demonstrating potential capability to destroy U.S. navigation satellites, the Soviets might be able to degrade the effectiveness of U.S. SSBNs on patrol.

To provide the leadership with a reservoir of men and material to replace the heavy losses anticipated from a major strategic exchange, the Soviets have developed a civil defense program. The Soviet civil defense organization is part of the Ministry of Defense and is headed by a general who is a deputy minister. The permanent full-time staff of the organization is reportedly more than one hundred thousand. Full-time civil defense staffs exist at each level of the Soviet administrative structure, from the central to the local level. Civil defense staffs also operate at key industrial and economic installations.

The specific goals of Soviet civil defense are to protect industrial capacity and to sustain the essential work force to enable economic recovery following an attack. In assessing Soviet effectiveness to achieve these goals, the U.S. Central Intelligence Agency (CIA) estimated the following:

> The Soviets probably have sufficient blast-shelter space in hardened command posts for virtually all the leadership elements at all levels. . . . Shelters at key economic installations could accommodate about 12 to 24 percent of the total work force. . . . A minimum of 10–20 percent of the total population in urban areas (including essential workers) could be accommodated at present in blast-resistant shelters. The critical decision to be made by the Soviet leaders in terms of sparing the population would be whether or not to evacuate cities. Only by evacuating the bulk of the urban population could they hope to achieve a marked reduction in the number of urban casualties. An evacuation of urban areas could probably be accomplished in two or three days, with as much as a week required for full evacuation of the largest cities.[28]

The Soviet civil defense system would be of limited effectiveness in protecting the general population, according to the CIA study. A worst case attack could kill or injure well over 100 million people. With several days of evacuation, casualties could be reduced by more than 50 percent; and with a week for preattack planning, "Soviet civil defenses could reduce casualties to the low tens of millions."[29]

According to a U.S. Department of Defense report, the Soviet civil defense system would be able to protect only 6–12 percent of the total work force at key industrial installations.[30] This report also noted that one key dimension of the Soviet effort to protect industry, namely its geographical dispersal, has not been implemented to any significant degree.

> New plants have often been built next to major existing plants. Existing plants and complexes have been expanded. No effort has been made to increase the distance between buildings or to locate additions in such a way as to minimize fire and other hazards in the event of a nuclear attack. Previously open spaces at fuel storage sites have been filled with new storage tanks and processing units. In sum, the value of overall production capacity has been increased proportionately more in existing sites than in new areas.[31]

In addition, this report also cast doubt on whether the widespread practice of hardening industrial installations as a means of protection would be effective. "Published civil defense guidelines acknowledge the high cost of such measures, and the Soviets appear to have given greater emphasis to the rapid shutdown of equipment and other measures that could facilitate longer term recovery after an attack."[32]

In spite of its limitations, the Soviet civil defense system would provide some protection for critical defense production assets by the sheltering of workers, the hardening of some economic installations, and the stockpiling of industrial and raw materials in protected areas. Without this system, the leadership would have little hope for the postattack force reconstitution effort which they apparently feel is essential to any possibility of prevailing in nuclear war.

As long as the central leadership remains alive, has accurate information with which to make decisions, and is able to communicate and to execute its decisions, it will attempt to use those elements of the surviving force structure and defense production assets in order to continue the war effort. In other words, the entire objective of strategic defense is to enable the Soviet leaders to have the option of force reconstitution in the postattack environment.

The ability to reconstitute forces and to direct them toward the fulfillment of military missions presupposes what Western military analysts call C^3 connectivity. Simply put, the central leadership must be able to send and to receive information, must be capable of processing that information rapidly, and must be able to communicate with a network of authoritative military, political, and economic decision makers throughout the country. Serious disruptions of the C^3 system would undermine the ability of the leadership to make effective decisions in a timely manner.

A critical dimension of C^3 connectivity is the receipt and processing of information for central decision makers concerning the damage inflicted on the Soviet Union and its strategic forces by the U.S. nuclear forces and vice versa. Such information would be necessary both in order to enter into negotiations and to retarget Soviet forces for subsequent strategic exchanges. The Soviets would hope to be able to retarget their remaining forces in order to threaten any U.S. military assets that might have survived an initial strategic exchange.

A potential dimension of the strategic force reconstitution effort would be the reloading of surviving strategic weapons platforms. The Soviets have tested their ICBMs in a refire mode and such capability would be especially useful to warfighting in the initial postattack environment. The Soviets have also developed resupply systems for reloading their SSBNs.[33] But without a survivable communication linkage between the surviving forces and the central leadership, effective targeting tied to political and military objectives would be virtually impossible.

The large military manpower and equipment reserves of the Soviet Union would be an additional element in the reconstitution effort. The Soviets have in peacetime a reserve force of more than 25 million of which some 5 million have served within the last five years. This means that the Soviet Armed Forces strength of nearly 4 million in peacetime could be more than doubled alone by reservists with recent military experience. The significance of a reserve pool would be increased in a postattack environment. In light of the devastation anticipated by both sides, the side that is able to augment its forces most quickly and effectively could gain the decisive initiative. The Soviets also retain a large pool of older military equipment, especially for the ground forces, which might be available to replace Soviet equipment losses. Even an inventory of old equipment would be formidable if the adversary was unable to match it.

The protection of defense industrial assets by civil defense methods would probably ensure the survival of at least some military production capability. Again what might be critical would be the ability of the Soviets to engage in defense production, even to a limited extent, if the adversary was unable to do so. The determination of the scope and nature of surviving defense assets, both in terms of forces and production assets, and the allocation of these assets to critical tasks requires that the central leadership be able to maintain C³ connectivity with military, economic, and political organizations throughout the country. Put in other terms, the Soviets regard the ability to mobilize military assets and to direct those assets against remaining adversarial forces as critical to the outcome of strategic war and as the major potential contribution of strategic defense.

The U.S. Strategic Force Posture

The United States and the USSR field quite different strategic offensive forces.[34] The Soviets emphasize the ICBM as the premier strike force while the SLBM is the most significant one for the United States. The long-range bomber plays only a peripheral role for the Soviets whereas it plays a significant one for the United States.

The largest number of U.S. strategic launchers are represented by the U.S. ICBM force of 450 Minuteman IIs, 550 Minuteman IIIs, and 33 Titan IIs (see Table 2.4). The first variant of the solid-fuel Minuteman series was originally deployed in 1963 but has been replaced by the Minuteman IIs and IIIs. The Minuteman II was an upgrading of the Minuteman I's capabilities rather than a radically new departure. The Minuteman II is a three-stage ICBM which carries a single thermonuclear warhead. In comparison with the earlier version, the

TABLE 2.4
U.S. ICBMs

Type	Number Deployed	Warheads per ICBM
Titan II	33	1
Minuteman II	450	1
Minuteman III		
With Mk-12 warhead	250	3
With Mk-12A	300	3

Source: Based on data obtained from Thomas Cochran et al., U.S. Nuclear Forces and Capabilities (Cambridge, Massachusetts: Ballinger Books, 1984).

Minuteman II is more accurate and carries a more sophisticated guidance system. This system is capable of prestoring the locations of a larger number of alternative targets which thereby increases targeting flexibility. The range, accuracy, and payload of the Minuteman II allow it to strike all but the most hardened military targets, namely, missile silos.

The Minuteman III is the most potent weapon in the U.S. strategic arsenal. Like the other Minutemans, the third variant is a three-stage ICBM powered by a solid-propellant rocket motor, but it incorporates significant advances, most notably the ability to carry multiple warheads. Most of the improvements relate to the final state and reentry system as well as the introduction of a MIRV system of three warheads. The MIRV system in effect is a fourth stage of the missile. The motors of this stage are controlled by a guidance package that directs the release of the warheads, chaff, and decoys from the reentry vehicle.

A further modification in the early 1980s of the Minuteman III has involved the fitting of more than 300 of the 550 launchers with the new (and more powerful) W-78 warhead, for the three Mk-12a reentry vehicles on each launcher. The high degree of accuracy of this warhead combined with the NS-20 guidance package gives these Minuteman IIIs a high kill probability against very hard targets, including Soviet ICBM silos.

The final ICBM deployed by the United States is the aging Titan II. Originally, fifty-four Titan IIs were deployed beginning in 1963, but two were lost in silo accidents in 1978 and 1980. The Titan II

TABLE 2.5
U.S. Nuclear Ballistic Missile Submarines and Missiles

Type of Submarine	Number Deployed	Type of Missile System	Number of Warheads per Missile
Lafayette	19	Poseidon C-3	10-14
Franklin	12	Trident C-4	8-14
Ohio	3	Trident C-4	8-14

Source: Based on data obtained from U.S. Department of Defense, Soviet Military Power (Washington, D.C.: Government Printing Office, 1984); The Military Balance 1983-1984 (London: International Institute for Strategic Studies, 1983).

is the largest U.S. ICBM and carries a single nine-megaton warhead. The main problem with the Titan II is its relatively low level of accuracy which results in limited hard-target kill capability. It is therefore unable to attack Soviet silos. Although close to retirement by the United States, the Titan II has been kept in service primarily because it is the only "heavy" U.S. ICBM in service.

The second largest number of U.S. strategic launchers is represented by the SLBM force of 568 missiles deployed on thirty-four operational SSBNs (see Table 2.5). The SLBMs, however, carry the bulk of U.S. strategic warheads. Currently, all but three of the thirty-four operational SSBNs are of the Benjamin Franklin/Lafayette Class. Each submarine of this class carries sixteen SLBM launching tubes. The U.S. Navy's thirty-one SSBNs of this class are armed with the Poseidon C-3 missile (nineteen SSBNs) and the longer range Trident I missile (twelve SSBNs).

The Poseidon is a two-stage solid-propellant strategic missile which is the successor to the first U.S. SLBM, the Polaris. Although the range of the Poseidon is the same as the Polaris, it has an increased capability to carry a large payload. Each Poseidon can carry up to ten warheads. Although there were originally thirty-one SSBNs of the Benjamin Franklin/Lafayette Class which carried Poseidons, twelve of these ships have been retrofitted with the longer range Trident I (C-4) SLBM. The range of the C-4 allows the SSBN so configured to have larger operating areas and shorter transit times from port to patrol areas. According to the 1983 Posture Statement of the chairman of the Joint Chiefs of Staff, "The Trident I creates a greater ASW problem for the Soviets, allows faster positioning for a fully-generated SSBN force, and provides the capability to attack the Soviet Union from all points of the compass rather than on the fairly limited and predictable axes of attack from ICBM bases."[35]

However, the Trident I was not just designed to increase the capabilities of an existing class of SSBNs. Rather, it was designed as the weapons system for an entirely new class of SSBN, the Ohio Class. By the end of 1983 the first three operational submarines of this class had been deployed. The Ohio Class is the largest U.S. SSBN and is significantly larger than the Soviet Delta Class SSBN. The Trident/Ohio Class program has been developed to deploy a strategic submarine capable of carrying a long-range missile (there is a Trident II missile under development that has one-third more range and much greater accuracy than the Trident I), of targeting the Soviet Union while cruising in remote open ocean areas, of incorporating state-of-the-art quieting technology (to make U.S. SSBNs harder to locate), and of having a high at-sea to in-port ratio (to be at sea at least 80 pecent of the time). Each Ohio Class SSBN has twenty-four SLBM tubes with each SLBM capable of carrying from eight to fourteen warheads.

Currently, the deployed Poseidon SLBMs carry more than three thousand warheads. In addition, the Trident SLBMs carry more than two thousand warheads. This means that there are nearly twice as many SLBM as there are ICBM warheads in the U.S. strategic arsenal.

The third type of strategic platform is the long-range or "heavy" bomber. Currently, SAC relies upon 272 B-52s to conduct strategic operations against the Soviet Union. Both the B-52s and the FB-IIIs are designed to conduct low-altitude operations against Soviet air defenses.

Until December 1982, U.S. strategic bombers relied on a mixture of highly accurate gravity bombs and somewhat less accurate short-range attack missiles (SRAMs) to attack Soviet targets. But as of December 16, 1982 the SAC bomber force added a new weapons system—the air-launched cruise missile (ALCM). Each B-52 in the initial squadron of sixteen was configured to carry twelve ALCMs in addition to an internal load of SRAMs and other weapons. The ALCMs are essentially pilotless bombs tipped with a nuclear warhead. Each ALCM has a pretargeted set of twelve target sites against which the pilot can choose to attack. Armed with the ALCM, the bomber pilot does not have to penetrate Soviet air defenses directly but can "stand-off" outside the range of the Soviet air defense network and launch the ALCM. According to the 1983 Posture Statement of the chairman of the Joint Chiefs of Staff, "The extremely accurate ALCMs are able to destroy the hardest Soviet targets. The ALCM's 2,500

TABLE 2.6
Estimated U.S. Strategic Nuclear Warheads

System	Number Deployed	Warheads per Launcher	Total Warheads
ICBM			
Minuteman II	450	1	450
Minuteman III	550	3	1,650
Titan	33	1	33
SLBM			
Poseidon C-3	304	10[a]	3,040
Trident C-4	216	8[a]	2,112
Subtotal (ICBM and SLBM):			7,285
Aircraft			
B-52D	31	4[b]	300
B-52G	123	8[b]	984
B-52G with ALCMs	28	12	336
B-52H	90	8[b]	720
TOTAL:			**9,625**

[a]May carry up to fourteen RVs.

[b]Assumes four gravity bombs and no SRAM for B-52D, four gravity bombs and four SRAM for B-52G/H; these are operational, not maximum, loadings. SRAM counted as deliverable warhead.

Source: Based on data obtained from The Military Balance, 1982-1983 (London: International Institute for Strategic Studies, 1982); The Military Balance 1983-1984 (London: International Institute for Strategic Studies, 1983); Thomas Cochran et al., U.S. Nuclear Forces and Capabilities (Cambridge, Massachusetts: Ballinger Books, 1984).

km range enhances targeting and routing flexibility and can reduce bomber exposure to current and projected Soviet air defense systems."[36] Currently, there are two squadrons of B-52s armed with ALCMs.

U.S. strategic forces, which are summarized in Table 2.6, would be directed by a C³ system that would transmit decisions made by the National Command Authority (NCA), i.e., the president or his duly designated successor. The U.S. system emphasizes the ability to inform the president of a pending attack and transmit his decision on how to respond. According to a Carnegie Endowment report on U.S. national security, the structure of the U.S. C³ system operates in the following manner:

> Early warning of an attack would be transmitted by radio links and land lines to a series of command centers. North American Air Defense Command (NORAD), located deep inside Cheyenne Mountain in Colorado, would evaluate the incoming data. NORAD would then confer with the National Military Command Center (NMCC) in the Pentagon and the SAC headquarters in Omaha, Nebraska, to verify an attack and assess its characteristics. Finally, the Chairman of the Joint Chiefs of Staff, the Secretary of Defense and the President would be notified. (A military aide, constantly with the President, has a briefcase containing nuclear retaliatory instructions and options.) This system is rehearsed regularly and the President probably could be informed promptly of any attack. The United States has developed several alternate command posts to provide redundancy for the President and top military commanders. The Alternate National Military Command Center (ANMCC) near Fort Ritchie, Maryland, could immediately assume the duties of the NMCC if the Pentagon were destroyed. The National Emergency Airborne Command Post (NEACP), one of four specially equipped Boeing 747s . . . could take the President or a designated successor aloft during a crisis. In addition, SAC and United States commands in Europe, the Atlantic, and the Pacific have airborne command posts. SAC's "Looking Glass" is maintained on continual airborne alert and is the center of a larger fleet of EC-135 aircraft (converted Boeing 707s) known as the Post-Attack Command and Control System (PACCS). NEACP and PACCS provide the facilities to command United States nuclear forces.[37]

Comparing U.S. and Soviet Strategic Offensive Forces

The simplest measure of the U.S.-Soviet strategic weapons inventory is to count the total number of delivery systems available to the two sides. The Soviets exceed the United States in numbers of strategic launchers. They have nearly 1,400 deployed ICBMs compared to slightly more than 1,000 for the United States. The Soviets have more than 900 SLBM tubes as compared to less than 600 tubes for the United States. Only in terms of strategic bombers does the United States exceed the Soviet Union.

A direct comparison of the delivery systems is of limited relevance, however, for it ignores the fact that almost all of these delivery systems carry several warheads that can be directed against separate targets. From the standpoint of the numbers of deployed warheads, the lesser number of U.S. delivery vehicles carry more warheads than do the greater number of Soviet ones. According to IISS figures, the United States has more than 9,000 warheads deployed to more than 7,000 warheads for the Soviets.

The distribution of warheads is quite different in the two arsenals. The vast majority of Soviet warheads are carried by ICBMs whereas for the United States the least number of warheads are carried by ICBMs. The greatest number of U.S. warheads are carried by submarines whereas less than 20 percent of Soviet warheads are on SLBMs. Long-range bombers carry the second greatest number of warheads for the United States whereas they carry the least number for the Soviets.

The two force structures can be further compared in terms of assessing the inherent military potential. A simple but very crude method of measuring inherent military potential is to compare throw-weights, i.e., the payload that the strategic launchers are capable of carrying. By this measure, the Soviets have more than 11 million pounds of throw-weight potential to more than 7 million for the United States. The lead in throw-weight is due almost entirely to the emphasis by the Soviets on the deployment of large ICBMs, especially the SS-18. In contrast, strategic bombers carry nearly half of the throw-weight in the U.S. arsenal. But this simple measure is very inadequate for it takes little account of a number of critical factors, such as the accuracy of the warhead, which have a significant impact on the destructive effect of any given payload.

A more sophisticated measure of inherent military potential has been provided by IISS. By developing an indicator called "equivalent megatonnage," it is possible to gain a rough comparison of the aggregate warhead yield in the strategic inventories.

A crude measurement of capability against area targets (such as cities and major military concentrations) is aggregate warhead yield, expressed in megatons. But destructive power does not grow proportionately with a simple increase in yield; a 10-MT weapon is not ten times as destructive as a 1-MT weapon. Hence, a more accurate indicator is "equivalent megatonnage" (EMT), which for a given warhead is usually expressed as the two-thirds power of its explosive yield or $Y^{2/3}$. Thus, the EMT of a 200-KT warhead is $(0.2)^{2/3}$ or (.34). However, EMT may overstate the effectiveness of very large weapons, because the area of potential destruction is likely to exceed the area of the target to be destroyed.[38]

According to equivalent megatonnage comparisons, the Soviets have roughly a 50 percent advantage over the United States in total. The

Soviets have an even more significant advantage (150 percent) over the United States if only ICBMs and SLBMs are considered.

A final assessment of inherent military potential is provided by comparing potential target coverage. There are basically two types of targets—area and point targets. Area (or soft) targets are places such as cities or major military concentrations. Point (or hard) targets are places such as hardened missile sites and hardened C³ centers. The destruction of point targets requires the use of much more accurate weapons than does area targets. A high degree of accuracy of delivery systems and their warheads are critical to overcome the hardness of protected sites.

The two strategic arsenals are quite different in terms of the mix of potential target coverage. The U.S. arsenal has more capability to destroy area targets, but the Soviet arsenal has more ability to destroy point targets in a time-urgent manner. The Soviets and the Americans have approximately the same ability to destroy point targets, but the delivery systems capable of attacking these targets are different. U.S. hard-target kill capability is contained in a joint bomber and ICBM force, whereas the similar Soviet capability is carried almost entirely by ICBMs. The result is that the Soviets have a significant advantage in time-urgent hard-target kill potential, i.e., in the warheads delivered by ICBMs against point targets.

The U.S. and Soviet strategic force postures can be further compared in terms of a number of vulnerabilities that would allow one to destroy a significant portion of the other's forces. But both would have enough forces remaining after a preemptive or surprise first strike to be able to deliver a powerful second strike, thereby providing a deterrent to the conduct of a preemptive strike.

ICBM Vulnerability

The United States has a more vulnerable ICBM force than does the Soviet Union, but given the large percentage of warheads carried by the Soviet ICBM force, vulnerability poses a problem for the Soviets as well. In order to assure a high probability of destroying a hardened ICBM silo, two high-yield and high-accuracy warheads must be employed. Only the U.S. Minuteman III and the Soviet SS-18 and SS-19 ICBMs carry warheads with the requisite yield and accuracy. The United States currently has approximately 1,500 warheads deployed on Minuteman IIIs; the USSR has over 4,000 warheads deployed on SS-18s and SS-19s.

The more than 1,000 U.S. ICBM silos could be targeted on a 2:1 basis and still leave the Soviets with more than 2,000 SS-18 and SS-19 warheads in reserve. In contrast, the more than 1,500 warheads on the Minuteman III could destroy only half of the nearly 1,400 Soviet ICBM silos. Hence, the Soviet Union has the potential to destroy the entire U.S. ICBM force with its ICBM force; the United States does not.

Nonetheless, even with the destruction of the entire U.S. ICBM force, the Soviets would have eliminated only 2,000 of the more than 9,000 warheads in the total U.S. inventory. The Soviets would have eliminated, however, the only U.S. time-urgent hard-target kill capability. In contrast, by killing 700 Soviet ICBM silos in a ICBM preemptive strike, the United States could eliminate up to 4,000 warheads, representing more than one-half of the total number of warheads in the Soviet inventory.

Of particular concern to the Soviets would be the more than 300 Minuteman IIIs armed with the highly accurate Mk-12A warhead and the NS-20 guidance system. One assessment of the counterforce potential of the U.S. ICBM force has been provided by the Congressional Budget Office (CBO).[39] According to the CBO, the current inventory of 550 Minuteman IIIs (assuming none were armed with the Mk-12A warhead) would be able to destroy more than 40 percent of the Soviet ICBM force. If all the Minuteman IIIs were armed with the Mk-12A warhead, nearly 60 percent of the Soviet ICBM force could be destroyed. The current mix of the two systems could consequently destroy nearly one-half of the Soviet ICBM force and with it nearly 40 percent of the total warheads on deployed Soviet systems.

A further concern in an ICBM exchange is the deployment locations of the respective ICBM arsenals. The Soviet ICBM fields cut through the largest concentration of the ethnic Russian population. According to Ball:

Unlike the United States, which has deployed her ICBMs generally in the center of the country, the Soviet ICBMs extend across virtually the entire USSR. A Soviet attack limited to the United States ICBM sites would fall completely east of 115°W longitude and west of the Mississippi River, and would be less difficult for United States early-warning and attack assessment systems to differentiate from an attack involving the major United States population and industrial centers and the national capital. A United States retalitory strike against the Soviet ICBM fields, on the other hand, must cover nearly the entire geographic expanse of the Soviet Union, including the more heavily populated and industrialized area west of the Urals. Processing data on some 1,000 to 2,000 warheads and other objects such as penetration aids and booster fragments targeted over this vast region might pose insuperable problems for the Soviet attack assessment system. This is especially the case vis-à-vis the three of four ICBM fields in the Moscow area.[40]

SLBM Vulnerability

The U.S. SSBN force is relatively more invulnerable than the Soviet SSBN force. But the Soviet SSBN force might be secure enough to assure its use in a second strike role. The survivability of the U.S. SSBN force is even more critical to the United States because one-half of all U.S. strategic warheads are sea-based. The survivability of the U.S. force tends to ensure U.S. ability to direct a devastating second strike against Soviet territory.

The relative invulnerability of U.S. SSBNs is based on three major factors. First, U.S. SSBNs are extremely quiet, providing little opportunity for Soviet acoustic sensors to detect them in the open ocean. Second, Soviet anti-submarine warfare capabilities in the open ocean are neither extensive nor effective. Third, the Soviets have very limited access to open oceans where most U.S. SSBNs operate.

Currently, the Soviets are unable to detect the location of the fifteen to twenty SSBNs that are on station in peacetime, and these submarines can stay at sea for extended periods. An additional 30 percent of the SSBN force could put to sea in a crisis; only 20 percent of the force would be left in port, vulnerable to Soviet attack.

A successful effort to attack SSBNs at sea requires the use of a large-area ocean surveillance system. Currently, the Soviets have no such system. Soviet problems are further complicated by the deployment of the new U.S. SLBM, the Trident. The long range of this missile dramatically expands the ocean area available for on-station patrol. The expansion of SSBN patrol areas greatly magnifies the difficulty for the Soviets of attempting to track and destroy U.S. SSBNs.

Suggestive of the difficulties confronting the Soviets in prosecuting U.S. SSBNs is their inability to effectively trail the SSBNs. According to Joel Wit, a research associate of the Georgetown Center for Strategic and International Studies:

> The most practical method to initiate a trail is simply to wait at base exits or at relatively narrow geographic choke points for these ships. Nuclear attack submarines, because of their speed and endurance, are considered the most effective ASW platforms for trailing. . . . [But] geography is a powerful constraint on the Soviets' ability to concentrate capabilities outside of American submarine base exits. The United States Navy recently ceased strategic operations at all of its overseas submarine bases except at Holy Loch, Scotland. The great distances between Soviet submarine and American SSBN bases make it extremely difficult for the Russians to attempt trailing on anything more than an occasional basis. This difficulty in attempting to station attack submarines near

base exits is compounded by the generally low peacetime Soviet submarine deployment rate of 10–15 percent.[41]

There is, however, one significant area of SSBN vulnerability of particular concern to the United States, namely the methods used to transmit and receive communications between the SSBN and the strategic command authority. According to the CBO report: "At the present time, submarines use an antenna close to or above the surface of the ocean for this purpose. As a result, a Soviet satellite system that could detect these antennas might pose a threat to the survivability of all or part of the submarine force."[42]

A further source of vulnerability is the in-port time for the SSBN force. In peacetime, according to the CBO report, about 55 percent of the Benjamin Franklin/Lafayette Class SSBN force is at sea. But in times of crisis this percentage could be raised to nearly 100 percent of submarines not in overhaul or, in other words, 80 percent of the total SSBN force could be put to sea in a crisis. The new Ohio Class SSBN will be able to maintain nearly a 70 percent at-sea deployment in peacetime, further eroding the ability of the Soviets to destroy U.S. SSBNs in port by means of a surprise attack.

The Soviet SSBN force is more vulnerable than the U.S. force on virtually all dimensions already discussed. Soviet submarines are significantly noisier than U.S. submarines which makes them easier to trail. U.S. ASW forces are significantly superior to those of the Soviet Union. The United States has an extensive open-ocean surveillance system which provides the United States with much greater capability to locate and destroy Soviet SSBNs. The Soviet deployment rate in peacetime is much lower than the U.S.'s (15 versus 55 percent) which leaves the bulk of the Soviet SSBN in port.

Nevertheless, ASW is a difficult process. According to the Carnegie Endowment report, "American ASW forces . . . are not capable of destroying all or even a substantial majority of the Soviet on-station SLBM force in a short span."[43] U.S. and NATO ASW advantages, however, might well come to the fore in a protracted war-setting where both sides might attempt to conduct anti-SSBN campaigns.

Long-Range Bomber Vulnerability

The problem of strategic bomber vulnerability is almost entirely a U.S. one; only the United States places heavy emphasis upon this type of weapons platform. The problem of bomber vulnerability is twofold. Bombers need to be able to survive an attack on their bases and they need to be able to penetrate Soviet air defenses to deliver weapons against their targets.

The major threat of a preemptive strike against U.S. bomber bases comes from Soviet SLBMs deployed off the U.S. coast. These SLBMs have flight times of only nine to twelve minutes. If these SLBMs could be launched on "depressed trajectories," they could reach U.S. bomber bases in less than ten minutes time. According to the Carnegie Endowment report, depressed trajectories refer "to flight paths of ballistic missiles fired at an angle to the ground significantly lower than standard launches. Such shots have short flight times and stay below line-of-sight radars longer than attacks along conventional arcs."[44] The Soviets, however, have not tested SLBMs in depressed trajectories.

There is no doubt that most bombers not on strip alert at the time of an SLBM attack would be destroyed. In peacetime, 30 percent of the U.S. B-52 force is maintained on ground alert, but in times of crisis the vast majority of the force could be placed on alert.

There are serious problems confronting any Soviet attempt to conduct a surprise attack directed against SAC bases. In order to minimize warning time, Soviet submarines would have to position themselves close to U.S. shores. Such a move would in most likelihood be detected by U.S. ASW sensors. Such detection would provide the United States with warning of an imminent attack. According to the CBO report:

> Since detection of provocative Soviet submarine deployments would enable the United States to put the entire bomber force on alert, an attempt to launch a surprise attack on alert bombers could be a counterproductive tactic. Furthermore, since a damage-limiting strike would probably be considered by the Soviet Union only in a time of extreme crisis, United States forces would almost certainly be in a high state of readiness at the time of an attack.[45]

After bombers have successfully escaped attacks on their bases, they must still be able to penetrate Soviet air defenses. To do so requires the bomber force to operate at low altitudes. The Carnegie Endowment report calculated that:

> At present, the bomber force could penetrate Soviet air defenses with acceptable losses. Their ability to penetrate projected Soviet air defenses of the 1990s, however, is expected to be very limited unless the United States wishes to expend a large number of ICBMs to suppress Soviet defenses. By that period, the Soviets will likely utilize advanced surface-to-air missiles, airborne warning and control system radars, and "look down-shoot down" interceptor aircraft capable of some radar detection and interception at low altitudes.[46]

The degradation of Soviet air defenses would not be the sole responsibility of the SAC bombers themselves. U.S. land- and submarine-based missiles would be used to destroy a large portion of Soviet air defense before the arrival of the bomber force. In addition, the ALCM-equipped bombers do not need to penetrate Soviet air space. These bombers rely upon the use of long-range cruise missiles, the low-level flight and small size of which would help them avoid detection and enable them to strike targets in the USSR.

In contrast to the U.S. bomber force, the Soviets have one that is smaller and far less capable. Long-range bombers comprise a small portion of Soviet nuclear forces. The Soviet force would be extremely vulnerable to a surprise attack, for these planes are not held on alert status in peacetime.

The Assured Destruction Mission as the Outcome of an All-Out Nuclear Exchange

In considering the vulnerability of strategic offensive forces it is not enough to consider the systems in isolation. The Carnegie Endowment report reminded us, "the combination of forces is stronger than the sum of its parts."[47] For example, it is difficult to surprise both the U.S. SAC bombers and ICBMs at the same time. The flight time of incoming ICBMs (thirty minutes) allows the bombers to take off. If SLBMs are used to attack bomber bases, the ICBMs are given warning of Soviet preemptive attacks.

Put in other terms, each part of the U.S. offensive strategic force would contribute to the survivability of the others. For example, the detection of the deployment of a large number of SSBNs close to U.S. shores would allow the United States to put a much larger portion of its bomber forces on peak alert, which would increase their chances of survivability. As a result of the synergistic quality of U.S. strategic forces, the CBO report concluded that "It is likely that an adversary interested in a counterforce strike against the United States would attack all three forces together. To do otherwise would only increase the damage that surviving American forces could inflict in a nuclear war."[48]

The Soviets rely for synergy on their array of offensive and defensive systems, rather than upon a diversity of offensive forces. The United States cannot currently destroy the Soviet ICBM force, although a first strike against Soviet ICBMs would significantly degrade the number of warheads available for war fighting. Given the inability of the United States to defend against the remaining Soviet ICBM warheads, the Soviets have an assured destruction capability in their ICBM arsenal. The Soviet SSBN force provides a further assured destruction capability against U.S. territory. Soviet Strategic defenses provide a key hedge against U.S. bombers and SLBM forces (assuming all U.S. ICBMs go against Soviet ICBMs). In light of the diversity of passive and active measures for strategic defense available, the Soviets would hope that the remaining U.S. strategic forces would be attrited by an attempt to overcome defensive measures and to thereby significantly reduce U.S. assured destruction capability.

In turn, the vulnerabilities of the U.S. strategic forces are not such as to impede the United States from delivering a strong retaliatory strike against the Soviet Union. If the Soviets preempted against U.S. ICBMs, SLBMs and bombers would receive warning time to respond. If bomber and submarine bases were attacked, ICBMs and SSBNs on patrol would receive a warning. If the Soviets attacked simultaneously all U.S. strategic forces, the United States could still respond with a significant force of surviving bombers and submarines as well as ICBMs launched while either under attack or upon confirmed warning.

There are at least two authoritative simulations in the unclassified literature of the effects of a Soviet preemptive strike on U.S. strategic forces. Both underscore the ability of the United States to deliver a devastating second strike in response to a Soviet first strike.

According to calculations by CBO using the Snapper (Strategic Nuclear Attack Program for Planning and Evaluation of Results) model developed for the U.S. Air Force by the Rand Corporation, the U.S. strategic triad could survive even a Soviet surprise attack in peacetime levels of alert and still deliver a devastating second strike.[49] In a comprehensive surprise attack on U.S. strategic forces in their day-to-day alert posture, Soviet SLBMs would target SAC bomber bases, and ICBMs would attack ICBMs and SSBN ports. Soviet SLBMs would destroy 70 percent of the B-52 force. The approximately 50 percent of the SSBN force in port would be destroyed. If the SS-18 force attacked U.S. ICBM fields, much of the U.S. ICBM force would be destroyed. Even after such a surprise attack, the United States would be left with virtually as many warheads as the Soviets had in the strategic reserve. The United States would have enough strategic warheads available to be able to destroy the Soviet Union. According to the CBO report:

Since 1,000 Poseidon SLBM warheads could destroy about 75 percent of the Soviet industrial targets (Trident warheads will be even more destructive), and since the same number of cruise missiles could destroy over 80 percent of the Soviet industrial base, the United States would have more than enough weapons in both the bomber and submarine parts of the triad to destroy the Soviet Union as a modern industrial society. Thus, given the survivability of at-sea submarines and alert bombers, a Soviet counterforce attack on United States ICBM silos, submarine ports, and bomber bases does not offer the prospect of successful damage limiting.[50]

If it is assumed that the strategic exchange occurred when U.S. forces were in a high state of readiness, i.e., in a generated alert posture, then at least 80 percent of the bomber force and 75 to 85 percent of the submarine base would survive a Soviet attack. The United States would be in a much better position under such conditions than when attacked in a day-to-day alert posture.

An even more authoritative assessment has been provided on an annual basis by the chairman of the Joint Chiefs of Staff in his Posture Statement. The 1982 report provided computed outcomes of four strategic force exchanges between the United States and the Soviet Union for 1979 through 1989. The mid-to-late 1980s trends incorporated projected U.S. deployments of a new ICBM (MX), the new Ohio Class submarines (with Trident I SLBMs), and the B-52s armed with ALCMs. "In each scenario, targeting goals for each side are assumed to be the same: first attacking all of the opponent's ICBM silos and shelters with nuclear weapons; and then, using weapons not allocated to that task, inflicting "moderate damage" to a specified percentage of the remainder of the opponent's target system. Perfect C^3 is assumed for both sides."[51]

The first scenario entailed an exchange in which the Soviet Union preemptively attacks, and the United States retaliates in kind after riding out the Soviet attack. Both sides are assumed to be in a normal, day-to-day alert posture at the start of the attack. In such an attack, the Soviets would have slightly more discretionary force potential (i.e., strategic forces that would remain after the attack) than would the United States.[52]

The second scenario entailed a Soviet-initiated exchange when both U.S. and Soviet forces are in a fully generated posture. In such a posture, all strategic systems would be in a high state of readiness (bombers dispersed, SSBNs on station, ICBMs at maximum alert). In this situation, the United States would have slightly more discretionary force potential than the Soviets after the Soviet attack.

The United States may choose not to ride out a Soviet attack, but, rather, to "launch under attack" (LUA), i.e., to launch its forces before the Soviet weapons arrive. The third scenario entailed a LUA by the United States with both sides on a day-to-day alert. The United States would have more discretionary force potential than the Soviet Union after such an attack. The effects of a LUA by the United States would be even more pronounced when both sides would be in a fully generated posture. The fourth scenario involved LUA in a fully generated posture. The U.S. advantage in discretionary force potential increases significantly under a LUA option. As the chairman of the Joint Chiefs of Staff noted, "Although the United States has no policy that assumes or requires LUA, the fact that the LUA option is available weighs heavily in any Soviet deliberations on the advisability of a preemptive strike."[53] The ability of the United States to respond to a Soviet preemptive strike after riding out an attack or by launching while under attack is a critical factor deterring the Soviets from wishing to fight an all-out nuclear war.

In other words, there is a high probability that the United States would continue to have a significant capability to inflict assured destruction on Soviet society even after a preemptive attack by Soviet forces. The "objective reality" of assured destruction in the event of an all-out nuclear war has had an important impact on the Soviet approach to war fighting, a subject to which we now turn.

Notes

1. The data in this chapter are taken, unless otherwise noted, from one of the following sources: *The Military Balance, 1983–1984* (London: International Institute for Strategic Studies, 1984); *The Balance of Military Power* (New York: St. Martin's Press, 1983); U.S., Department of Defense, *Soviet Military Power* (Washington, D.C.: Government Printing Office, 1981, 1983, and 1984); Robert P. Berman and John C. Baker, *Soviet Strategic Forces: Requirements and Responses* (Washington, D.C.: The Brookings Institution, 1982); Ronald T. Pretty, ed., *Jane's Weapon Systems, 1982–1983* (London: Jane's Publishing Co., 1982); U.S., Department of Defense, *NATO and the Warsaw Pact: Force Comparisons* (Washington, D.C.: Government Printing Office, 1981); *Challenges for U.S. National Security* (Preliminary Report) (Washington, D.C.: Carnegie Endowment for International Peace, 1981); *Challenges for U.S. National Security* (Third Report) (Washington, D.C.: The Carnegie Endowment for International Peace, 1982).

2. Berman and Baker, *Soviet Strategic Forces*, pp. 5–13.

3. *Challenges for U.S. National Security* (Third Report), pp. 133–134.

4. Ibid., p. 133.

5. *Soviet Military Power*, 1984, p. 26.

6. Desmond Ball, *Can Nuclear War Be Controlled?* (London: International Institute for Strategic Studies, 1981) (Adelphi Paper #169), pp. 43–45.

7. *Soviet Military Power*, 1984, pp. 40–41.

8. Berman and Baker, *Soviet Strategic Forces*, p. 100.

9. Ibid., p. 124.

10. *Soviet Military Power*, 1981, p. 56.

11. Ibid.

12. John Erickson, "The Soviet View of Deterrence: A General Survey," *Survival* (November-December 1982), p. 248.

13. *Soviet Military Power,* 1984, p. 23.

14. Berman and Baker, *Soviet Strategic Forces,* p. 20.

15. Ibid., p. 130.

16. Ibid., p. 95.

17. Ball, *Can Nuclear War Be Controlled?,* p. 45.

18. Gordon MacDonald, Jack Ruina, and Mark Balaschak, "Soviet Strategic Air Defense," in Richard K. Betts, ed., *Cruise Missiles: Technology, Strategy, Politics* (Washington, D.C.: The Brookings Institution, 1981), p. 67.

19. *Soviet Military Power,* 1984, p. 36.

20. Ian Bellany, "Sea Power and the Soviet Submarine Forces," *Survival* (January-February 1982), p. 6.

21. Norman Polmar and Norman Friedman, "The Soviet Navy: Their Missions and Tactics," *Proceedings (of) U.S. Naval Institute* (October 1982), pp. 34–44.

22. *Soviet Military Power,* 1984, p. 21.

23. Ibid., p. 33.

24. *Aviation Week and Space Technology* (April 1984), p. 49.

25. *Soviet Military Power,* 1984, p. 34.

26. Ibid.

27. *Challenges for U.S. National Security* (Third Report), p. 119.

28. U.S., Central Intelligence Agency, Director of Central Intelligence, *Soviet Civil Defense,* NI 78-10003, July 1978, pp. 2–3.

29. Ibid., p. 31.

30. U.S., Department of Defense, Annual Report, 1981 (Washington, D.C.: Government Printing Office, 1980), p. 78.

31. Ibid.

32. Ibid., p. 79.

33. *Soviet Military Power,* 1984, p. 22.

34. The data in this section is taken unless otherwise noted from one of the following sources: *The Military Balance, 1983–1984; The Balance of Military Power; Jane's Weapons Systems, 1982–1983; NATO and the Warsaw Pact; Challenges for U.S. National Security* (Preliminary and Third Reports); U.S., Department of Defense, Chairman of the Joint Chiefs of Staff, *Military Posture Statement* for 1982, 1983, and 1984.

35. *Military Posture Statement,* 1983, p. 72.

36. Ibid., p. 74.

37. *Challenges for U.S. National Security* (Third Report), pp. 94–95.

38. *The Military Balance, 1982–1983,* p. 138.

39. U.S., Congressional Budget Office, *Counterforce Issues for the U.S. Strategic Nuclear Forces* (Washington, D.C.: Government Printing Office, 1978).

40. Desmond Ball, "Research Note: Soviet ICBM Deployment," *Survival* (July-August 1980), p. 169.

41. Joel S. Wit, "Are Our Boomers Vulnerable?" *Proceedings (of) U.S. Naval Institute* (November 1981), p. 67.

42. *Counterforce Issues*, p. 26.

43. *Challenges for U.S. National Security* (Third Report), p. 83.

44. Ibid., p. 40.

45. *Counterforce Issues*, p. 27.

46. *Challenges for U.S. National Security* (Third Report), p. 41.

47. Ibid., p. 39.

48. *Counterforce Issues*, p. 27.

49. Ibid., pp. 57–73.

50. Ibid., p. 28.

51. *Military Posture Statement*, 1982, p. 26.

52. Ibid.

53. Ibid., p. 29.

3
The Soviet Approach to the Conduct of Nuclear War

Soviet military analysts have written a great deal about the "unthinkable." They have confronted directly the challenge that the conduct of a nuclear war would present to the Soviet Union. In this chapter, we will provide an overview of what Soviet military analysts have said and what the Soviet force structure suggests about the probable nature of nuclear war and how the Soviet Union might best prepare to fight it.

The recognition by Soviet political and military leaders of the destructiveness of an all-out nuclear war underscores the need for an effective military strategy, rather than making the formulation of strategy unnecessary. As David Holloway of the University of Edinburgh put it:

> The destructiveness of nuclear war has been strongly emphasized in the Soviet press. . . . At the same time, however, it is asserted that such a war has to be prepared for: strategy, in other words, has not been made redundant. Parity has been affirmed by Brezhnev as the goal of Soviet policy, and the pursuit of superiority has been disavowed. Parity is a key concept here, for it approximates to the idea of mutual deterrence in that it recognizes that for the time being the basic nature of the Soviet-American strategic relationship is one of mutual vulnerability to devastating retaliatory strikes. But parity does not carry two of the most important connotations of mutual deterrence: it does not suggest that the nuclear balance is a fool-proof mechanism for preventing war, and it does not imply that war should not be prepared for.[1]

An effective military strategy is one designed to win an armed conflict. This requirement is no different for the U.S.-Soviet nuclear war than any other kind of war. Nonetheless, the unprecedented character of such a war would clearly affect the nature and meaning of victory.

Victory cannot be defined in a global nuclear war as the rapid destruction of the adversary with little or even minimal damage to oneself. Losses would be heavy on both sides in such a conflict. Victory would be the ability to prevail over the adversary in the context of a catastrophe of global proportions.

Nonetheless, the concept of victory is not perceived by Soviet military analysts to be meaningless in the strategic nuclear age. It would undercut the importance of maintaining and developing Soviet military power postured directly against the United States and NATO if victory was held to be impossible. The point of view of Soviet military analysts is to discuss military developments in terms of improving the ability to win any war, including a strategic nuclear conflict.

Victory combines military and political goals. Militarily, victory is possible if the adversary's military forces and capabilities can be destroyed while minimizing one's own military losses. Politically, victory is possible if one can use the remaining military forces to seize enemy territory to aid in the process of postwar recovery. The goal of Soviet strategy would be to attain such a victory in the event of nuclear war.

Put in other terms, victory remains a meaningful concept in a nuclear war to the extent to which one can destroy the adversary's military forces and his military potential at acceptable cost. In this sense, the Soviet approach is a "counterforce" strategy. The Soviets emphasize the need to be able to destroy the adversary's military capability, rather than destroying wantonly the adversary's civilian population. In short, Soviet strategy emphasizes the significance of destroying the adversary's military forces, minimizing losses to one's own forces, and effecting a postwar recovery (especially on a European-wide basis).

Nonetheless, the high degrees of risk and uncertainty to Soviet forces and to the Soviet homeland associated with the conduct of nuclear war cannot be eliminated. Risk and uncertainty remain very high in the context of confronting a powerful adversary such as the United States which possesses a formidable strategic arsenal. But risks can be reduced by having an effective military strategy. The reduction of risk in one's favor to the disadvantage of one's adversary and the ability to dominate the ladder of escalation is the heart of the Soviet approach to formulating an effective strategy to fight a nuclear war.

The development of a military strategy designed to reduce the risks to one's own forces at the expense of the adversary's is hardly an enthusiastic affirmation of the desirability of fighting a nuclear war for political gain. Although Soviet military writers affirm with ritualistic certitude that socialism will prevail in a strategic war, they do not spell out in detail anywhere the fruits of such a victory. They do not indicate what would make fighting such a war a desirable (as opposed to a potentially necessary) exercise from the Soviet point of view. In fact, the absence of any serious discussion by Soviet military writers of the positive benefits derived from fighting a nuclear war clearly calls into question the desirability of ever fighting such a war except under the most extreme circumstances.

The Military Requirements of Nuclear War Fighting

The unprecedented nature of a U.S.-Soviet nuclear war requires careful prewar thinking and preparation to ensure that one will be at an advantage from the outset. Soviet military writings are part of such an effort and represent the most vocal manifestation of Soviet preparation to fight a nuclear war. As such, these writings (almost all taken from the Brezhnev period) underscore a number of key requirements in forging a viable strategy for conducting a strategic war.

Survivable Command and Control Capability

A very basic requirement for nuclear war fighting is to develop a survivable command and control capability. This capability is necessary in order to sustain military operations in the disruptive conditions of the nuclear battlefield. As Colonel M. Shirokov underscored, "Under conditions of a nuclear war, the system for controlling forces and weapons, especially strategic weapons, acquires exceptionally great significance. A disruption of the control over a country and its troops in a theater of military operations can seriously affect the course of events, and in difficult circumstances, can even lead to defeat in a war."[2]

One critical dimension of the command and control problem is the direction of strategic nuclear forces. Without a survivable command and control system for strategic forces only a policy of massive retaliation is possible. Any controlled or measured use of strategic weapons would require the existence of a viable command and control system. The construction of redundant command and control centers is considered by Soviet analysts to be critical to the viability of strategic power. Also, command and control centers are considered very lucrative targets for strategic strikes. For example, Major General Kh. Dzhelaukhov has indicated that "points for the control and guidance of strategic nuclear means" are among the highest priority targets for a strategic attack.[3]

The importance of command and control to strategic war fighting cannot be overemphasized. Command and control is essential to ensure that one is not devastated by a surprise strategic strike. It is also necessary to have viable command and control systems to ensure that one's own strategic forces are directed to destroy the critical enemy targets. Admiral S. G. Gorshkov underscored the importance of command and control to strategic war fighting in these words:

> Under today's conditions when opposing groupings of forces have nuclear weapons at their disposal which are essentially sufficient to destroy completely one another many times over, control of forces is related to the employment of various automated equipment to ensure surprise and swiftness of operations and to gain time over the enemy. In this case, control of forces is a guarantee of success. It has become especially critical in the realm of the employment of nuclear forces and the forces whose mission it is to knock them out.[4]

A second dimension of the command and control problem is to maintain direction over the battlefield situation in the various theaters, but especially in the European theater. The complexity of the problem is given by the combined arms character of modern warfare. Highly mechanized units are designed to conduct a rapid advance, including large numbers of tanks. A diversity of aircraft performing various missions (ground attack and support, air-to-air combat, strategic bombing, and aerial reconnaissance) have to be coordinated with the ground attack. Naval support both in terms of blunting the enemy's naval-to-shore attacks (by means of aircraft, missiles, or artillery) and in terms of supporting ground assault operations must be closely coordinated with ground and air forces. The nuclear factor adds an important wrinkle to this already difficult problem. Nuclear weapons can destroy both command posts and communications networks. In light of the critical need to coordinate a combined arms operation, the havoc that well-targeted nuclear weapons can create is essential to defeating the enemy. As Colonel V. Savel'ev and Colonel P. Shemanskii have noted, the problem of command and control under modern conditions has become especially acute "since the capabilities of [both] sides to disrupt control has increased by far in connection with the launching of nuclear strikes against troops and control posts."[5]

A third dimension of the command and control problem is to maintain direction over one's force structure to ensure the ability to continue pursuing military objectives. The shift from the use of conventional to nuclear weapons will be decisive if a U.S.-Soviet strategic war begins with a short or prolonged conventional phase. It is essential to ensure that one is not caught off guard by a surprise theater or strategic nuclear strike by the enemy, for such an attack could seriously degrade one's nuclear or conventional capabilities. Major General N. Vasendin and Colonel N. Kuznetsov have noted that the United States

> does not exclude the possibility of opening military operations even in the main theaters, with the use of just conventional means of destruction. Such a beginning of war can create favorable conditions for the movement of all nuclear forces to regions of combat operations, bringing them into the highest level of combat readiness, and subsequently inflicting the first nuclear strike with the employment in it of the maximum number of missile launch sites, submarines and aircraft at the most favorable moment.[6]

Command and control connectivity is crucial to ensure the ability to order one's nuclear strikes in the most effective manner possible, i.e., precisely after the enemy has massed his conventional and nuclear strength but before he has launched nuclear weapons.

The Element of Surprise

The second basic requirement for nuclear war fighting is effectively dealing with the element of surprise. The tremendous destructive power that strategic weapons can deliver in a very short period of time is the basis of the problem of surprise in modern warfare. Colonel V. V. Larionov has underscored that "the first surprise nuclear missile strikes can cause unprecedented destruction, exterminate tremendous numbers of troops in places of their usual quartering, and destroy a significant part of the populations of large cities."[7] If one could carry out a surprise strategic attack, decisive victory might be possible.

Deterring the enemy from having such a possibility of decisive strategic success is the preeminent challenge for Soviet strategic forces. Lieutenant General Gareev observed that "the most important task of the Soviet Army and Navy (since the 1970s) has been to prevent a surprise nuclear attack and to ensure annihilation of the aggressor if he dared initiate a war against our country."[8]

The difficulties in delivering a preemptive strike as well as the nature of the challenge of preventing a surprise nuclear attack have been well articulated in a major article on surprise attack in modern warfare. According to Major General Vasendin and Colonel Kuznetsov the following conditions are critical to the execution as well as the prevention of a surprise strategic attack:

> Any aggressor risks unleashing a nuclear war only with confidence of achieving victory. And confidence in the success of a nuclear attack can occur in conditions whereby there is a sufficiently high guarantee that

nuclear strikes will be delivered to the objectives of destruction, that a mass launch of ballistic missiles and takeoff of aircraft will occur for a relatively long time undetected by the country against which the attack is being carried out, and that the armed forces, and above all the strategic nuclear means of the enemy, will suffer such destruction that they will be incapable of carrying out a powerful retaliatory nuclear strike. In order to eliminate the possibility of such a favorable situation for the aggressor and deprive him of the temptation to risk the unleashing of a nuclear war, it is necessary to maintain strategic nuclear means in constant high combat readiness, dispersed and well concealed, and to have a reliable system of early warning of a mass launch of strategic missiles and takeoff of strategic aircraft, as well as effective means of combating the nose cones of ballistic missiles and the aircraft of the enemy.[9]

The elements of a successful preemptive attack are clearly set out by these two Soviet analysts. First, there has to be a high degree of confidence in the performance capabilities and accuracy of one's strategic weapons in an actual combat situation. Also significant in this regard is a high degree of confidence in one's reconnaissance capability. It is critical to be able to locate all of the major strategic systems of the adversary in a timely fashion just prior to launching one's strategic systems. Without highly effective reconnaissance, strategic weapons are blinded. Second, there has to be a high degree of confidence in the inability of the adversary's reconnaissance to pick up the attacking strategic systems. Presumably this confidence could be rooted in a judgment that the adversary's reconnaissance systems are of low technical quality or that one has degraded the adversary's reconnaissance capabilities sufficiently so that a significant part of the attacking strategic forces will get through to enemy targets undetected, or that he will be deprived of sufficient warning time to act. Third, there has to be a high degree of confidence that a sufficient degree of destruction of the adversary's force structure will occur so that the enemy will be unable to deliver a powerful and devastating second strike.

The elements of effective protection against being caught off guard by the enemy's strategic attack are also identified by the two analysts. First, one's strategic forces must be kept at high levels of combat readiness. There is virtually no mobilization time possible for strategic forces to be launched in retaliation. They must be constantly ready to go. Second, one's strategic forces must be as survivable as possible. Survivability is enhanced by dispersal and concealment of strategic systems so that the targeting problems of the adversary are severely complicated. Third, one must have very effective reconnaissance capability. It is necessary to be able to detect and to verify extremely quickly that an adversary has launched his strategic weapons. Fourth, one must have effective anti-ballistic missiles and anti-aircraft missile systems to be able to destroy a significant number of the enemy's incoming strategic missiles and bombers.

The Soviets would clearly hope in the context of a strategic war to be able to go first or to preempt U.S. strategic forces. The advantages of a successful strategic surprise are irresistible. But the very conditions that make retaliation possible for the Soviets also make it possible for the Americans. Hence, the treatment of strategic surprise in Soviet military thought tends to revolve around the tactics for achieving the highest degree of surprise possible in a strategic war. Dispersing strategic systems, camouflaging strategic systems, and attacking the enemy's reconnaissance systems are among the favorite tactics discussed in Soviet writings to maximize the ability of the Soviets to go first in a strategic war.

Combined Arms Operation

The third basic requirement of nuclear war fighting is the ability to conduct a successful combined arms operation. This will be very difficult in the context of the unprecedented levels of disruption associated with the use of nuclear weapons in the European battlefield.

One basic dimension of the battlefield problem is to adopt appropriate military tactics. For example, Soviet analysts emphasize that it is critical to concentrate ground and air power to defeat the enemy on the European battlefield. According to Colonel M. Popov, the need to concentrate troops is required because "the attainment of superiority in combat power over the enemy is provided in certain circumstances primarily by the concentration of superior forces."[10] But the concentration of forces provides a lucrative target for enemy nuclear strikes. The need to disperse troops is required to avoid "the danger of destruction of troops concentrated in a relatively small area by the nuclear weapons of the enemy."[11] Popov suggested that it is necessary to combine judiciously the concentration and dispersal of forces as phases in response to a fluid battlefield situation. "During military operations, to carry out a certain strategic, operational or tactical mission, troops may be forced to concentrate, according to a previously worked-out plan for the shortest possible period."[12]

Another important tactic is to direct forces along an axis of attack rather then massing them along a front. If there is a conventional phase preceding strategic strikes, it is critical to attack along an axis in order to protect oneself against nuclear attack. As Colonel N. Kalachev noted "When an offensive operation is conducted with the use of exclusively nonnuclear weapons, it is considered possible to achieve the essential preponderance over the defending force only as a result of resolute and fast massing of men and equipment on specific axes selected for breaching the defense with their subsequent rapid dispersion."[13] The introduction of nuclear weapons into combat enhances the need to attack along lines of axis without providing excessively lucrative targets for nuclear strikes. According to Colonel I. Liutov, in a nuclear battlefield situation it is necessary to concentrate the "main efforts on a main axis, and particularly the bulk of nuclear firepower, as well as in rapid exploitation by the troops of the results of nuclear strikes."[14]

A second basic dimension of the battlefield problem is the creation of a flexible and mobile conventional force structure able to implement the tactics appropriate to the fluid conditions of the nuclear battlefield. As Lieutenant General V. Reznichenko underscored, combined arms combat in the nuclear age is "a combination of nuclear strikes and maneuver-emphasizing actions by large units and subunits of various arms and services, coordinated in objective, time and place."[15] The conventional arm must be built around "maneuver-emphasizing" forces capable of rapidly exploiting the results of nuclear strikes. There must be especially close coordination between ground and air forces to ensure the development of a rapid offensive. Ground attack aircraft are a critical element in ensuring the ability of the mechanized armed forces to advance rapidly in destroying the enemy's conventional and tactical nuclear forces impeding the advance. Air superiority is necessary in order to block the enemy from using his power to attack Soviet offensive thrusts. NATO intends to rely significantly on helicopters and ground attack aircraft to slow the tank forces of the Warsaw Pact. NATO's air capability must be seriously degraded to ensure a rapid offensive by the Warsaw Pact.

It is critical as well to develop a strong "forward detachment" capability in offensive operations. Colonel I. Vorb'ev underscored the significance of "comparatively small, highly mobile and maneuverable detachments, which have been assigned concrete tasks [which] may broadly utilize intervals and gaps in the defense and, without engaging in combat with enemy forces, can much more rapidly reach the designated objectives and support operations of their main forces."[16] These forward detachments can be especially useful in destroying the enemy's tactical nuclear systems, in destroying the enemy's command and control systems, and in seizing strategic areas in the enemy's rear.

A third basic dimension of the battlefield problem is to use tactical nuclear weapons correctly. On the one hand, it is crucial to be able to control the process of escalation to the use of tactical nuclear weapons. Colonel B. Samorukov characterized the challenge of the transition from conventional to nuclear weapons in the following manner:

> Above all, attention must be devoted to the fact that constant readiness of both sides for the use of nuclear weapons is dangerous; that one of them can precede the other in the infliction of a nuclear strike. This will force the opponents to organize and carry out their combat operations with conventional means of destruction in such a way as to be in the most favorable position in relation to each other in case of the use of nuclear weapons, to acquire an advantage in nuclear means, to be ready for a rapid offensive immediately after nuclear strikes, and to have the necessary dispersal of troops for the purpose of protection from means of mass destruction.[17]

On the other hand, it is crucial to be able to use tactical nuclear weapons in close coordination with conventional forces on the European battlefield to attain military objectives with the least amount of collateral damage possible.

Furthermore, it is critical to be able to maximize the ability to use one's own military reserves and to minimize the enemy's ability to do so. As Major General Kh. Dzhelaukhov noted, "Intensifying strategic efforts by employing strategic reserves of the second strategic echelon is a most important factor in waging a successful struggle to achieve strategic objectives under modern conditions."[18] The continual provision of troops and material resources for a European war requires that the Soviets be able to transport goods and manpower within the European continent. In contrast, NATO's strategic reserve is the United States. The Soviets place special importance upon reducing the ability of NATO to be able to draw upon this strategic reserve if there is a protracted war. Especially important in this regard would be the ability of the Soviet Navy to disrupt NATO resupply efforts at sea. Rear Admiral V. Andreev underscored that military operations on the ocean will be of great significance in World War III. This is due in part to "the increased importance for the imperialist states of ocean communications for the supply of all the necessary strategic groupings."[19]

Strategic Defense

The fourth basic requirement of nuclear war fighting is to maximize the possibilities for strategic defense. Strategic defense is conceived of by the Soviets as a critical adjunct to successful strategic offensive. As Colonel I. Grudinin underscored, the failure to execute a strategic defense would result in the lack "of a capability to carry out the strategic offensive, for there would be nothing, or nobody to carry it out. It is, therefore, impossible to underestimate the value of civil defense which, given present day conditions as a whole, has, beyond doubt, taken on a strategic significance."[20]

The first form of strategic defense is ballistic missile defense. Soviet analysts are well aware of the current technological limitations of ballistic missile defense systems. They emphasize the importance of an active research and development program to prevent the United States from having a technological advantage in this area. They also emphasize the importance of maintaining a deployed system to provide protection for Moscow. But they recognize the primacy of offensive weapons at this period in the development of strategic forces. Such Soviet recognition was a key reason for their willingness to conclude the ABM treaty with the United States in 1972.

The second form of strategic defense is anti-submarine warfare. ASW is necessary to degrade the enemy's attack submarine force to increase the ability of Soviet strategic nuclear submarines to survive at sea throughout a protracted war period. Soviet naval officials are well aware, however, of the difficulties facing Soviet ASW forces attempting to degrade U.S. SSBNs. But they are also well aware of the need to have the ability to protect their SSBN systems from attack to preserve their war reserve role.

A third form of strategic defense is air defense. The Soviets have placed great emphasis upon air defense to protect Soviet military facilities from hostile bomber attack. Soviet analysts have underscored the flexibility that bombers have in attacking mobile targets. They are especially concerned to degrade NATO bomber capability in order to be able to protect Soviet lines of supply and communication from the Soviet Union to Europe. The significance of air defense was well articulated by the head of the national air defense command, Marshal P. Batitskii:

> In the past, air defense handled the mission of securing protection against air attack only for major installations and positions within range of hostile aircraft, while today the main task of the national air defense troops is defense of major political and administrative centers, industry, power resources, lines of communication, the civilian population, troops and important military installations throughout the country, as well as protection of mobilization measures.[21]

A fourth form of strategic defense are "passive" defense measures designed to protect major "reserve" industrial facilities. For example,

Major General A. Kornienko and Captain V. Korolev asserted that "complete annihilation of the military economic might of large states from the outset of a war is hardly practicable. Reliable concealment and dispersal of industrial sites ensure their viability and ability to produce on certain scale."[22] Given the significance Soviets attach to the role of reserves in fighting a protracted war, such passive defense measures are considered critical to the prosecution of a successful war effort by ensuring the continued flow of supplies to the front.

A fifth form of strategic defense is the protection of the civilian population and the close integration of civilian defense with military needs in wartime. For example, General O. Tolstikov noted that a successful war effort will require the continued functioning of the transportation system under very difficult conditions. Civil defense forces can play a major role in ensuring the continued operation of transportation facilities. "Damaged bridges, railroad centers, and other communication installations can be quickly restored by civil defense forces."[23] The "close, continuous coordination of civil defense with the armed forces" will be critical to the outcome of the war effort.

In short, the four basic requirements of nuclear war fighting constitute the building blocks for a Soviet strategy to conduct nuclear operations. The key to an effective strategy is to be able to meet as many of these requirements as possible. Soviet analysts, however, are well aware of how difficult it would be to meet these requirements in a real war setting.

A Ladder of Escalation in the Soviet Force Structure

The Soviets might follow a limited nuclear war fighting approach in a war with the West. In such an approach, the Soviets would hope to keep the level of escalation below the all-out exchange level and to do so in such a manner as to ensure as favorable a war termination process as possible. The whole purpose of the strategic force posture would be to give the Soviet leaders various military instruments to deter the United States from further escalation and to make the United States unwilling to escalate to the level of an all-out exchange. The fear of such escalation would hang over both sides as they maneuvered vis-à-vis one another in the dynamic situation of a war in Europe. Political will as much as military capability would come into play and be tested. Potentially, the Soviets might be able to coerce a U.S. leadership unwilling to risk further escalation but willing to negotiate an end to armed conflict. The formidable array of nuclear weapons at the disposal of the Soviet leadership avails them of at least such possibilities.

Much of Soviet declaratory policy denounces escalatory thinking on the grounds that any use of nuclear weapons will lead, inevitably, to an all-out nuclear war. But such declaratory policy is part of deterrence in a prewar setting for the Soviets. As Nathan Leites of the Rand Corporation argued, "It is perhaps just because the Soviets are so interested in the distinction between deterrence and warfighting that they have kept silent about it. The war not being yet begun, this is the hour of deterrence: deterrence by the prospect of a maximum initial strike, of preemptive, and of the none-or-all character of nuclear war. Once the war is on, the authorities may adopt that 'controlled' conduct about which the West [talks]."[24]

In actual fact, the Soviet arsenal provides the potential for limited strikes. The reason for Soviet interest in limited or controlled strikes would be precisely to lower the level of damage from a strategic war by avoiding the all-out exchange. Leites commented:

> Just because damage from strategic nuclear war is likely to be so high one should make maximum effort to limit that damage, as well as to procure (unlikely as it may be) gain from the outcome of such a war. That seems to be . . . the attitude in the Kremlin—an attitude to which those who hold it probably do not even conceive a "serious" alternative. To use a Western word, every level of damage appears "acceptable" if it cannot be reduced, even one *bordering* on "annihilation"—and not *being* that, radically *different* from it. Conversely, even a modest level of damage is "unacceptable" if it can be avoided.[25]

In this section we will briefly outline an array of scenarios in a ladder of escalation. The scenarios would range from the use of nuclear weapons in the European theater to an all-out strategic war.

Level One: Nuclear Weapons
on the European Battlefield

The Soviets might contemplate the use of various types of nuclear weapons on the European battlefield. The Soviets might use their short-range battlefield nuclear weapons (Frog 7, Scud B, SS-21, SS-23, or nuclear-capable self-propelled artillery) to attack NATO ground forces, especially NATO's short-range battlefield weapons. The basic political objective would be to raise the level of damage on West German territory and to thereby encourage West Germany to pressure NATO for an early end to nuclear hostilities.

The Soviets might go further and use their long-range theater nuclear forces (LRTNF) systems (especially their aircraft such as the Fencer and Backfire) to attack high-value NATO military targets in Europe. Among key NATO targets to be struck would be airfields, ports, and tactical missile and warhead sites. In addition to the obvious military objectives of such an attack, there are a number of political objectives served as well. The Soviets would be pressuring NATO for an end of hostilities prior to conducting significant strategic attacks directly against the territory of the European nuclear powers, Britain and France. A subordinate goal might be to try to "neutralize" France and Britain in order to undercut the will or need for France and Britain to use their strategic weapons against Soviet territory.

Finally, the Soviets might use their IRBM's (SS-4s or SS-20s), ICBMs (especially SS-11s), and/or theater ballistic missile submarines (Gulf and Hotel Class SSBNs) to attack French land-based nuclear systems and territory and/or British territory. The Soviets would also conduct an extensive ASW effort against French and British SSBNs. The objective would be to eliminate completely NATO Europe's military power and to thereby allow the Soviets to dominate Europe politically. The Soviets would do this with high expectations of British and French strategic reprisals. By taking even significant losses the Soviets might hope to increase their leverage over the United States by demonstrating a willingness to take losses prior to direct attacks on U.S. territory.

Level Two: Strategic Maneuver
Prior to Attack on U.S. Territory

The Soviets might attempt various strategic maneuvers, none of which would involve directly striking U.S. territory. The Soviets might carry out a massive urban evacuation. By using their civil defense system, the Soviets would try to gain a bargaining edge over the United States. By reducing the vulnerability of selected segments of their population, the Soviets would hope to reduce the significance of U.S. soft-target superiority. By carrying out an urban evacuation, the Soviets would demonstrate resolve and greater willingness to use their strategic offensive forces.

Nevertheless, any advantages the Soviets might obtain by urban evacuation might well be short lived. As Douglas Englund of the office of the chairman of the Joint Chiefs of Staff cautioned, "In the long run, by evacuating their cities, the Soviets may simply swap an immediate problem for a larger one."[26] According to Englund, a massive Soviet evacuation "would be detected by United States intelligence resources shortly after it was begun—thus allowing the

United States to initiate a counter-evacuation."²⁷ Englund further noted that U.S. evacuation capabilities are much greater than is usually assumed.

> One of the factors the Soviets would have to consider is that there are well over 100 million privately owned automobiles in the United States (compared to about 4 million in the Soviet Union)—or roughly one automobile for every two Americans. Consequently, the United States, although lacking the railroad capacity of the Soviet Union, could put virtually every citizen on the road in private autos. Americans have several other advantages. Typical United States families could stock their automobiles with enough extra clothing, food, and tools to enable them to subsist in a rural reception area until such time as the flow of goods and services could be rerouted. The United States road network is far more suitable than the Soviet Union's for moving large numbers of evacuees quickly and for distributing them throughout the rural areas. The climate of the United States is also comparatively more conducive to a crisis evacuation. And, finally, distribution of goods and services to United States rural areas is immeasurably better developed than in the Soviet Union. Thus, the Soviet analyst could easily conclude that (1) we could start later than the Soviet Union and still complete an evacuation before they could, and (2) an evacuated United States population would be in a comparatively more sustainable position.²⁸

The Soviets might contemplate another alternative to striking U.S. territory. The Soviets may attempt to degrade seriously the main U.S. strategic force, namely the SSBN force. The Soviets could use bombers delivering nuclear depth charges, nuclear attack submarines (SSNs) armed with nuclear torpedos, or ICBMs striking in the general area of a U.S. SSBN (which had been identified by Soviet ASW forces). By reducing the U.S. strategic reserve at sea, the Soviets would be able to demonstrate their ability to reduce U.S. strategic capabilities without directly attacking U.S. national territory. The Soviets would expect the United States to retaliate against Soviet SSBNs at sea, but given the greater reliance of the United States on SSBNs, even a roughly equivalent level of loss would be to Soviet advantage. The Soviets have, however, only a limited ability, at this time, to conduct a successful ASW campaign against U.S. SSBNs.

Nonetheless, the United States might well not play by Soviet escalatory rules. The United States might conduct a nuclear strike against prime Soviet submarine bases in the Kola Penninsula and at Petropavlosk, thereby seriously degrading the operational capability of the Soviet SSBN fleet. The United States might respond in terms of: "if you attempt seriously to degrade my strategic reserve at sea, then anything I do to accomplish the same end is legitimate."

Finally, the Soviets might use their anti-satellite capability to attack a variety of U.S. satellites, especially reconnaissance and SLBM targeting satellites. The U.S. satellite system represents a relatively small number of high-value targets, because the United States concentrates so many diverse functional capabilities in each individual satellite. By degrading U.S. C^3 systems in space the Soviets could reduce U.S. capabilities without attacking U.S. territory. Nevertheless, the United States could respond by launching replacement satellites into orbit with the space shuttle or could preemptively strike ASAT launch sites in the USSR.

The broad purpose of a massive evacuation, SSBN degradation, or space warfare would be to erode U.S. strategic capability and at the same time show Soviet willingness to escalate. But without directly attacking U.S. territory, the Soviets would hope to influence the United States to engage in a war termination process favorable to the Soviets.

Level Three: Limited Strikes Using Central Systems

Soviet strategic offensive forces are diverse enough to contemplate a variety of limited strikes against U.S. strategic systems. The threat of immediate escalation, however, would hang over any limited strike against U.S. central systems.

The Soviets might consider attacking U.S. strategic bomber bases in order to eliminate them as sanctuaries on U.S. territory for extended war fighting. The flexibility of the U.S. heavy bomber force is of concern to the Soviets. A portion of the U.S. bomber force could be used in the conventional phase of the war and to deliver nuclear weapons against European theater targets. Most of the strategic bomber force would, however, be kept in reserve to perform the strategic strike mission against Soviet territory. The elimination of the use of U.S. territory for bomber strikes against non-Soviet Warsaw Pact targets might well be a key goal for a Soviet strike against U.S. bomber bases. In addition, the destruction of the strategic bomber force would seriously reduce U.S. hard-target capability, i.e., the ability of the United States to strike Soviet ICBM and hardened C^3 sites.

For such an attack on U.S. bomber bases to remain limited, the Soviets might well have to attack with a small force of ICBMs or long-range SLBMs (on Delta Class submarines) in order to allow the United States to discern that the strike was indeed limited in character. The relatively long flight times of ICBMs and SS-N-18s would potentially allow the United States the time to identify the limited nature of the strike. Alternatively, the Soviets might use the "hot line" to inform Washington directly of the limited nature of the strike against U.S. bomber bases.

The Soviets might consider a limited attack against an urban area (other than Washington, D.C.) to demonstrate the willingness of the Soviets to escalate. The Soviets would hope that the devastation from this attack on a single city would paralyze the public with fear of the consequences of a general attack. Fear could then be translated into pressure on the U.S. leaders to end the war. Even if the United States retaliated in kind, the Soviet leaders would not be under the same pressure from its public. However, the Soviets might be under a different type of pressure equally significant to a war termination process. The Soviet nationalities problem might be seriously exacerbated under conditions of U.S. attack on a demonstration Soviet city. The possible dismemberment or unravelling of the Soviet empire in response to a NATO strike on a key Soviet city was hypothesized by some NATO generals in a speculative work, *The Third World War*. The destruction of the British city of Birmingham by the Soviets led to a NATO decision to destroy the city of Minsk. Two SSBNs, one U.S. and one British, launched two missiles each on the city of Minsk.

> This nuclear exchange, carried out on the Soviet side with no pretense of consultation with their subject allies let alone with the regional republics of the USSR, proved to be the trigger which set off the smouldering nationalist explosion. The growth of disaffection and resistance in Asia and in Eastern Europe [was intensified by the U.S.-Soviet strategic exchange]. . . . Now finally the realization [spread] that Russia might well have initiated a nuclear war which could engulf them all unless they immediately separated themselves from Russian control. The outbreaks were quicker and more violent in the East, more subtle but more decisive in Europe.[29]

Level Four: Central Systems Strikes Leading to
Massive Exchange

The Soviets might consider a preemptive strike against U.S. ICBMs, but would probably do so with high expectation of precipitating a massive response. Such a Soviet expectation would rest on the size of the attacking force needed to conduct a strike as well as the collateral damage from such a strike. The Soviets would need to expend at a minimum more than 4,000 warheads in such a strike. They would have to use the entire SS-18 force and almost all of the SS-19s as well. It would be extremely difficult and probably impossible for the U.S. C^3 system to distinguish such a "surgical" strike against U.S.

ICBMs from a massive strike. The collateral damage would be high as well, with U.S. estimates ranging from 1.6 to 50 million casualties.[30]

The purpose of a Soviet ICBM preemptive attack would be to degrade seriously U.S. time-urgent hard-target kill capability. If the Soviets could preemptively destroy the U.S. ICBM force (a proposition many U.S. strategic analysts question), they would be able to protect their ICBM force against a U.S. time-urgent preemptive attack. They would, however, remain vulnerable to a U.S. bomber attack if that force had not been already destroyed previously.

As an alternative to an ICBM preemptive strike, the Soviets could conduct a nuclear decapitation strike against U.S. C³ targets. According to Ball:

> Despite the increased resources that the US is currently devoting to improving the survivability and endurance of command-and-control systems, the extent of the relative vulnerability remains enormous. The Soviet Union would need to expend thousands of warheads in any comprehensive counterforce attacks against US ICBM silos, bomber bases and submarine facilities, and even then hundreds if not thousands of US warheads would survive. On the other hand, it would require only about 50–100 warheads to destroy the fixed facilities of the national command system or to effectively impair the communication links between the National Command Authorities and the strategic forces.[31]

Given the vulnerabilities of C³ systems and their location (Washington, D.C., and key strategic forces locations), the Soviets would probably not attempt to destroy these systems except in the context of a massive exchange. In fact, the connectivity or survivability of C³ systems is the prerequisite for the ability to conduct limited strategic strikes at all.

Level Five: Massive Strike

The Soviets might begin a massive strike with SLBM attacks against soft C³ centers. Soviet Yankee Class submarines, according to U.S. General J. Ellis, "routinely patrol off our coasts and have been known to approach close enough that, in the event of an attack, the resulting short SLBM flight time would greatly reduce the amount of warning time available to national decision-makers."[32] The Soviets could use the Yankee SLBMs to attack critical satellite ground terminals and early-warning radar facilities as well as the very low-frequency communication stations used to link SSBNs on patrol with the National Command Authority. In addition, a small number (ten to twenty) of high-altitude detonations could disrupt high-frequency communications and generate an electromagnetic pulse (EMP) over millions of square miles. Many of the most complex C³ systems, including power networks, computer facilities, and the airborne command and communications systems are quite vulnerable to EMP effects.[33]

The Soviets could attack other C³ sites such as the National Military Command Center (NMCC) with forward deployed SLBMs but the major underground command posts—the alternative NMCC in Maryland and the North American Air Defence (NORAD) and SAC command posts in the Midwest—would have to be targeted with Soviet ICBMs. Attacks on hardened C³ facilities would be part of a general ICBM strike.

The Soviets might have forward deployed a number of Delta Class SSBNs to areas off U.S. coasts to give their SLBMs a shorter flight time to attack bomber bases with greater chance of success. The SLBMs could also be used to strike other soft military targets, especially military bases and depots.

Concurrently with the launching of the SLBM attacks, the Soviets would launch a general ICBM attack. The SS-18 and SS-19 would be targeted against U.S. ICBM silos. The SS-11s, SS-13s, and SS-17s would be used against other military targets, including bomber bases, military bases and depots, and U.S. defense industrial assets.

Soviet SSBNs that remained in bastions in waters contiguous to the Soviet Union and long-range bombers could potentially be used in follow-on strikes. Such strikes would be targeted after the Soviets had determined through various reconnaissance means which sites were inadequately damaged. Such follow-on strikes could be spaced closely after the initial attack (e.g., bombers could be launched at the time of the ICBM attack and given orders in transit for final target destination) or several days after the strike, especially by SSBNs on patrol. The ability to use surviving strategic forces in a protracted strategic exchange would depend upon how well the Soviet C³ system survived a U.S. counterstrike. Although the Soviets have built a very redundant and potentially survivable C³ system, they cannot be absolutely certain of the ability of the system to function adequately in a postattack environment. As John Steinbrunner of the Brookings Institution noted:

> Although the Soviets have made extensive investments in measures to protect their command systems and, whether by intention or necessity, have utilized relatively primitive communications equipment significantly less sensitive to nuclear weapons effects, the consequence of their systematic attention to the subject appears to be an awareness of exposure rather than confidence in secure protection.[34]

After suffering from the inevitable U.S. retaliation, the Soviets would attempt to reconstitute their force structure, including remaining strategic weapons. They would hope to win what Leites called the "Restoration Race":

> The side that wins this race, wins the war. . . . Other things being equal, the Restoration Race is won [in the Soviet view] by the side entering it with the larger conventional reserves. Because after the missile nuclear strikes it will be necessary to crush the enemy's conventional forces and to occupy his territory, and because these tasks must be done primarily by ground forces, superiority, one may say, will remain with the side that will have preserved reserves. As the Restoration Race proceeds, so does the Race for the Prevention of the Enemy's Restoration. If both the pertinent resources of the two sides and what one might call their combat actions have been similarly depleted and degraded by the initial period of nuclear war, one effort of each side . . . is to utilize the scarce time during which the enemy's combat production function has not yet been restored to deplete his resources further. It is during this period that it is possible *rapidly* to inflict losses on the enemy which cannot be made good.[35]

Nonetheless, the need to engage in the Restoration Race is a mark not of the success of the Soviet military effort, but of its failure. The Soviets hope to deter escalation from the level of an all-out nuclear exchange. The purpose of having credible forces on the conventional and theater nuclear levels is to terminate the war on favorable terms prior to a need for the United States and the Soviet Union to suffer heavy losses on their national territories. The inability to deter such losses would represent a failure of Soviet military policy, or, alternatively, the need to succeed in ever more stringent and dangerous circumstances.

Notes

1. David Holloway, *The Soviet Union and The Arms Race* (New Haven, Connecticut: Yale University Press, 1983), p. 167.

2. Colonel M. Shirokov, "Military Geography at the Present Stage," *Voennaia Mysl'* 11 (1966), trans. in *Foreign Press Digest*, (hereinafter *FPD*), 0730-67, July 27, 1967, p. 63.

3. Major General Kh. Dzhelaukhov "The Infliction of Deep Strikes," *Voennaia Mysl'* 2 (1966), trans. in *FPD*, 0763-67, August 9, 1967, p. 43.

4. S. G. Gorshkov, "Nekotorye voprosy razvitia voenno-morskogo iskusstva," *Morskoi sbornik* 12 (1974), p. 28.

5. Colonel V. Savel'ev and Colonel P. Shemanskii, "Assuring the Stability of Troop Control," *Voennaia Mysl'* 8 (1968), trans. in *FPD*, 0019-70, March 30, 1970, p. 21.

6. Major General N. Vasendin and Colonel N. Kuznetsov, "Modern Warfare and Surprise Attack," *Voennaia Mysl'* 6 (1968), trans. in *FPD*, 0005-69, January 16, 1969, p. 45.

7. V. V. Larionov, in *Problemy revoliutsii v voennom dele* (Moscow: Voenizdat, 1965), p. 452.

8. Lt. General Gareev, "Ever Guarding the Achievements of October," *Voenno-istoricheskii zhurnal* 11 (1970), trans. in *Joint Publications Research Service*, 70538, January 25, 1978, p. 58.

9. Vasendin and Kuznetsov, "Modern Warfare and Surprise Attack," p. 46.

10. Colonel M. Popov, "The Laws of Armed Conflicts Are the Objective Basis of the Leadership of Combat Operations," *Voennaia Mysl'* 10 (1964), trans. in *FPD*, 914, May 20, 1965, p. 23.

11. Ibid.

12. Ibid.

13. Colonel N. Kalachev, "Attack Without the Employment of Nuclear Weapons," *Voennaia Mysl'* 2 (1973), trans. in *FPD*, 0045, November 20, 1973, p. 93.

14. Colonel I. Liutov, "Massing of Forces and Weapons in the Course of Combat Actions," *Voennaia Mysl'* 11 (1972), trans. in *FPD*, 0049, December 3, 1973, p. 59.

15. Lt. General V. Reznichenko, "Tactics—A Component Part of the Art of Warfare," *Voennaia Mysl'* 12 (1973), trans. in *FPD*, 0048, August 20, 1974, p. 40.

16. Colonel I. Vorob'ev "Forward Detachments in Offensive Operations and Battles," *Voennaia Mysl'* 4 (1965), trans. in *FPD*, 957, June 4, 1966, p. 15.

17. Colonel B. Samorukov, "Combat Operations Involving Conventional Means of Destruction," *Voennaia Mysl'* 8 (1967), trans. in *FPD*, 0125-68, August 26, 1968, p. 29.

18. Major General Kh. Dzhelaukhov, "Combatting Strategic Reserves in a Theater of Military Operations," *Voennaia Mysl'* 11 (1964), trans. in *FPD*, 924, June 30, 1965, p. 5.

19. V. Andreev "The Subdivision and Classification of Theaters of Military Operations," *Voennaia Mysl'* 11 (1964), trans. in *FPD*, 924, October 23, 1964, p. 18.

20. Colonel I. Grudinin, "Comment," *Voennaia Mysl'* 8 (1965), trans. in *FPD*, 958, April 22, 1966, p. 37.

21. Marshal P. Batitskii, "The National Air Defense Troops," *Voennaia Mysl'* 11 (1973), trans. in *FPD*, 0049, August 27, 1974, p. 34.

22. Major General A. Kornienko and Captain V. Korolev, "Economic Aspects of Soviet Military Doctrine," *Voennaia Mysl'* 7 (1967), trans. in *FPD*, 0120-68, July 30, 1968, p. 30.

23. Colonel General O. Tolstikov, "Civil Defense in Nuclear-Rocket War," *Voennaia Mysl'* 1 (1964), trans. in *FPD*, 939, August 4, 1964, p. 36.

24. Nathan Leites, *Soviet Style in War* (New York: Crane, Russak and Co., 1982), p. 379.

25. Ibid.

26. Lt. Colonel Douglas M. Englund, "The Selling of Soviet Civil Defense," *Joint Perspectives* (Summer 1980), p. 19.

27. Ibid.

28. Ibid., pp. 19–20.

29. General Sir John Hackett et al., *The Third World War: August 1985* (New York: Macmillan Publishing Co., 1978), pp. 304–305.

30. Desmond Ball, *Can Nuclear War Be Controlled?* (London: International Institute for Strategic Studies, 1981) (Adelphi Paper #169), p. 27.

31. Ibid., p. 35.

32. As quoted in Ball, *Can Nuclear War Be Controlled?*, p. 14.

33. On the C³ vulnerability problem see Ball, *Can Nuclear War Be Controlled?*, pp. 9–25.

34. John Steinbrunner, "Nuclear Decapitation," *Foreign Policy* (Winter 1981–1982), p. 20.

35. Leites, *Soviet Style in War*, pp. 372–373.

4
Soviet Perceptions of the
U.S. Military Challenge
to Strategic Parity

In this chapter we address the difficult question of whether the Russians believe they could attain strategic superiority and we attempt to answer this question indirectly by examining Soviet perceptions of the U.S. nuclear challenge. Soviet analysts of the United States tend to underscore the strengths of the United States in "accelerating" the arms race. U.S. scientific and technological virtuosity is an especially significant factor in regard to U.S. ability to "break out" in the arms race. As one group of Soviet analysts commented, "American ruling circles have not oscillated in their determination to direct the scientific-technological revolution as a political force, with the goal of ensuring American military-technical superiority over the Soviet Union."[1]

Technological dynamism makes the strategic balance tenuous. For example, V. M. Kulish maintained that the U.S.-Soviet strategic balance can be characterized only as "an approximate parity," because technological levels are not constant: "They are in continuing motion and are subject to periodic fluctuations and changes in favor of one side or the other. There is every reason to view this balance as a correlation between the strategic nuclear missile might of the two great powers at the present time, and also as a continuing process in the further development of this might."[2] Significantly, Kulish added: "The appearance of new types of weapons could seriously affect the balance of military forces between the two world systems. . . . Far-reaching international consequences could arise in the event that one side possessed qualitatively new strategic weapons."[3] To dispel any possible doubt about which side he expected to try to produce such weapons, Kulish concluded:

Even a relatively marginal and brief superiority by the United States over the Soviet Union in the development of certain "old" or "new" types and systems of weapons could significantly increase the strategic effectiveness of American military force, exert a destabilizing influence on the international political situation throughout the entire world, and create very unfavorable consequences for the cause of peace and socialism.[4]

The Kremlin has been and continues to be concerned with the possibility that the United States might achieve a major technological breakthrough in the strategic arms race for which the Soviets would have no credible response in a timely fashion. This concern with U.S. technological virtuosity is suggestive of Soviet expectations that they could not win an all-out strategic arms race.

In order to understand Soviet evaluations of the U.S. nuclear challenge, this chapter will examine recent Soviet commentary on the evolution of U.S. strategic policy since 1945. A reconstruction of the Soviet standpoint is provided to enable the reader to become familiar with Soviet views on the evolution of U.S. strategic policy over the past forty years.

1945–1961: U.S. Nuclear Monopoly and Massive Deterrence

The development by the United States of the atomic bomb during the latter stages of World War II had a profound impact on the development of U.S. military policy, according to Soviet analysts. U.S. leaders became convinced—particularly since the Soviet Union did not possess such a weapon—that they had developed an "absolute weapon" to form the bedrock of U.S. military policy. At the same time, the process which led to the development of nuclear weaponry led U.S. leaders to believe that the key to the future position of the United States in the world lay in the maximum utilization of its superior scientific-technical capabilities.[5] As a result, U.S. strategic planners decided to utilize the atomic bomb—or the threat of it—as a vital element in its foreign policy while at the same time making military-technical progress the foundation upon which future U.S. strategic policy would be based.

From the very beginning of the postwar period, U.S. possession of atomic weapons was primarily designed to intimidate the USSR, Soviet analysts maintain. In discussing the U.S. decision to use atomic weapons against Japan, for example, a Soviet analyst argued: "Merely to intimidate the Soviet people and their government, the American imperialists dropped atomic bombs on two cities in Japan which destroyed and doomed hundreds of thousands of peaceful inhabitants to severe suffering from radioactive contamination."[6]

U.S. reliance on advanced technology in its strategic policy vis-à-vis Moscow continued to be emphasized in the immediate postwar period. One Soviet analyst cited statements made in 1945 by U.S. Generals G. Marshall and H. Arnold on the importance of technology in strategic policy.[7] Another analyst referred to a 1946 Joint Staff document reportedly stating that U.S. strategy toward the Soviet Union must be based on "advanced military technology."[8]

U.S. policymakers tended to believe that their atomic monopoly would continue for some time in the postwar period. But the United States decided not to take any chances and introduced in 1946 the Baruch plan for nuclear disarmament to protect the U.S. monopoly. The plan called for the establishment of an International Control Organization over which the United States expected to exercise decisive influence. This organization was authorized to control the research, production, and utilization of explosive nuclear material. As one Soviet analyst put it: "It was unrealistic to think that the USSR and other states would agree to place all of its atomic industry under international—in essence American organizations—and reconcile itself with what is supplied to it in accordance with conditions set by the United States."[9] Furthermore, Soviet analysts maintain, until a control system would have been actually instituted, the United States would have been free to produce and accumulate nuclear weapons.[10] The plan, in the words of one Soviet analyst, constituted "an attempt to ensure American monopoly over the control of atomic weapons. As a result, the Baruch plan was rejected."[11]

Moscow's explosion of its first atomic bomb in 1949 had a major impact on U.S. strategic policy. Although the development of the Soviet atomic bomb did not eliminate Soviet scientific and technological inferiority vis-à-vis the United States, it did mark a change from a situation of U.S. nuclear monopoly to one of a "lead" in a nuclear arms race.[12] While Washington continued to be seen as strategically superior, its absolute superiority was eliminated.

According to Soviet analysts, the United States reacted to Moscow's explosion of its first atomic bomb with the publication of a secret memorandum—SNB-68/2—which, among other things, called for a buildup of conventional and nuclear forces as well as foreseeing the use of U.S. nuclear weapons against the USSR and its allies.[13] In addition, the United States intensified work on a new weapon—the thermonuclear bomb—which was successfully tested in 1952. The next year, however, the Kremlin detonated its own thermonuclear bomb. For the Soviets, only their ability to match U.S. strategic developments provides them with a reliable guarantee of deterring the United States.[14]

Throughout the 1950s, the United States relied on a basic geographical asymmetry to deter the Soviet Union. From bases surrounding the Soviet Union, the United States could strike the USSR with nuclear weapons. U.S. reliance on its asymmetrical capability to strike the Soviet homeland coupled with dynamic weapons developments provided the United States with the foundation for its doctrine of massive retaliation. According to one Soviet analyst, the doctrine of massive retaliation enunciated by the Eisenhower administration in 1954 embodied three basic assumptions, namely, maintaining U.S. technical superiority in systems in which the United States held a decisive lead, producing weapons capable of neutralizing the opponent's offensive or defense weapons, and possessing an overall military-technical superiority that would permit Washington to act from a "position of strength." By acting from such a "position of strength" the United States would be able to maintain superiority in economic, political, psychological, and ideological areas.[15]

In the Soviet view, Washington hoped to take advantage of Moscow's inferiority in delivery systems by adopting a strategic doctrine the primary purpose of which was to intimidate the USSR by threatening the massive use of intercontinental weapons against Moscow anytime "communist aggression" occurred anywhere in the world.[16] In practical terms, this meant a further buildup in U.S. long-range bomber and missile systems.

The ability of the United States to develop the massive retaliation doctrine rested in Soviet eyes upon the inability of the Soviet Union to strike the U.S. homeland with sufficient strength. The Soviets placed great emphasis upon the need to develop their capability to strike the United States with massive force in order to undercut the massive deterrence doctrine and the political blackmail it entailed.

The launching by the Soviet Union of its Sputnik in 1957 together with its steady buildup of long-range bombers and missile systems are viewed by Soviet analysts as important elements in solving the problems of ensuring Soviet ability to inflict massive destruction on the United States.[17] Throughout the nuclear age, the Soviet Union has placed as a sine qua non of a successful Soviet strategic policy the ability to inflict massive damage on the U.S. homeland in order to undercut U.S. geographical advantages vis-à-vis the USSR.

According to Soviet analysts, Moscow's enhanced strategic capabilities led U.S. strategists to question the appropriateness of the massive retaliation doctrine. Such a strategy was only credible as long as the United States was able to maintain an "absolute superiority" in strategic systems. Soviet advances not only raised questions about the extent—if any—of Washington's lead in this area, it also meant that the United States itself was not invulnerable in the case of a nuclear war. As one leading Soviet analyst put it: "It was necessary to come to the conclusion that the military-technical possibilities of the socialist countries and the existing correlation of forces in strategic weapons was such that American civilization itself could be put in question in case of a nuclear war by the United States against the USSR."[18]

Hence, from the Soviet perspective, by 1960 a major Soviet goal had been achieved. Massive retaliation had been eliminated as a viable mode of operation in U.S. foreign policy through the Soviet ability to inflict massive destruction on the U.S. heartland. The U.S. monopoly in nuclear weapons had been broken and the vulnerability of the United States to Soviet strategic systems in case of nuclear war established.

Nevertheless, the Soviets remained concerned about the technical and numerical inferiorities of their strategic systems. Although U.S. strategic planners had been forced to recognize the need to rethink the premises upon which their strategic doctrine was based, they continued to believe that U.S. technological sophistication and ability to outproduce the USSR in numbers of missiles and other strategic systems provided a sound basis for the further development of U.S. strategic power.

1961–1968: The Democrats and Flexible Response

The backbone of U.S. strategic power in the 1950s was the bomber fleet and the intermediate range ballistic missiles located on bases surrounding the Soviet Union. In the 1960s, the United States significantly increased its strategic power by deploying two new systems—Minuteman ICBMs and Polaris SLBMs. The development of these new systems symbolized U.S. scientific and technological strength. The Minuteman system represented a major breakthrough in solid-fuel propellant technology as well as an increase in guidance systems capabilities. Also, the Polaris system represented the state of the art in submarine technology, enabling these submarines to operate quietly and out-of-range of Soviet anti-submarine forces at the time.

In addition to developing new strategic systems, the Kennedy administration reformulated U.S. strategic doctrine. The flexible response strategy emphasized the need to develop a wider range of war-fighting options than simply relying on the threat of all-out nuclear war. Lawrence Freedman, a Western analyst, characterized the shift to flexible response in the following manner:

> Multiple options would mean that any American action could be tailored to the particular Soviet challenge. The choice would be greater than suicide or surrender. In an uncertain world where the contingencies were many, multiple options should mean that the Americans would not be caught unawares and unprepared. . . . The reason for the shift was straight-forward. Since Dulles' time there had been a declining interest in transforming any war into a nuclear contest. It was no longer as arguable that the United States would enjoy any significant advantages in such a context. The extension of options essentially meant a greater number and variety of conventional forces and indicated a United States readiness to fight solely conventional wars.[19]

Although the United States recognized that the use of strategic weapons might well lead to the destruction of the United States, the Soviets still felt that the U.S. threat of using such weapons remained an important political tool to be used against the USSR.[20] Now, however, the threat had to be commensurate with the political objectives to be attained. Rather than the first weapons threatened to be used, strategic systems would be the last rung on a ladder of escalation designed to protect U.S. interests. Consequently, the flexible response doctrine not only provided for the use of military force under special conditions, but also gave strategic systems an important, although somewhat indirect, role. In essence, Soviet analysts underscore that the doctrine of flexible response signified U.S. recognition of the irrationality of an all-out nuclear war. Strategic nuclear systems would now be used solely as a deterrent "in case of a war with a primary opponent."[21] At the same time, increased emphasis would be placed on the use of conventional forces on a global basis. The use of such forces would reduce the danger of a local conflict "escalating from the level of a local conflict to the level of 'central' nuclear systems."[22]

The conceptual underpinning of flexible response was guaranteed destruction. According to one Soviet observer, Secretary of Defense Robert McNamara in the Kennedy administration defined guaranteed destruction in terms of the need to maintain U.S. "strategic forces at a sufficient state of readiness in order to inflict unacceptable damage on any aggressor."[23] In practice, the U.S. administration interpreted this to mean that the United States should have the capability at a minimum to be able to destroy 20–25 percent of the Soviet population and 50 percent of its industry.

This strategy appeared to Soviet analysts to be partly consistent with McNamara's opposition to the acquisition by the United States of a first strike capability (i.e., the ability by the United States to deliver a disarming strike against the USSR while suffering only minimal damage in return). In fact, it was McNamara who argued in 1964 that any attempt by either side to deliver a first strike would lead to the mutual destruction of both sides.[24]

Nonetheless, it seemed to at least one Soviet analyst that in order for U.S. strategy to be effective, the United States would have to have "nuclear forces significantly more powerful than those of the Soviet Union."[25] McNamara called for the United States to produce a limited counterforce capability to supplement guaranteed destruction. He hoped that by having an ability to destroy a number of significant military and industrial targets through the deployment of the Minuteman ICBM that the USSR could be convinced "to enter into a mutual renunciation [with the United States] of the use of nuclear strikes on the territory of the other, or if that fails, to avoid hitting cities."[26]

From the Soviet vantage point, this amounts to the advocacy of a first strike doctrine. When combined with the concept of assured destruction the development of counterforce capabilities "was not compatible with strategic defense. No matter how it is presented, it only has a meaning if made into a preventive first strike."[27] After all, the same writer noted: "When one side prepares an unexpected disarming strike the other side is put into a position of unconditional strategic vulnerability, and for the other side there remains no other choice besides striking first at the side preparing a preventive strike."[28] Furthermore, Soviet analysts underscore that the United States did not rule out the possibility of a first strike under certain conditions in the doctrine of flexible response.[29]

While the theory of flexible response seemed challenging enough, it was the nature of the strategic systems developed by the United States in the 1960s that concerned the Soviets more. Propelled by the combined pressures of overcoming the perceived "missile gap" and the need to develop weapons systems that would give life to the new flexible response doctrine, the Kennedy administration put considerable emphasis on expanding its strategic weapons programs. In devising its strategic weapons systems, the Kennedy administration emphasized both quantitative and qualitative factors. According to Soviet analysts, the administration believed that despite the progress the Soviet Union had made, the USSR stood little chance in an all-out strategic nuclear competition with the United States, particularly in light of Washington's stronger economic base. Such competition could be made even more difficult for Moscow if it was channeled in the direction of advanced technological systems where the United States was believed to have a significant lead.[30]

From the Soviet standpoint, the announcement by President Kennedy on January 30, 1961, which called for an acceleration of the Polaris construction program, was a first step in accelerating the arms race in the 1960s. In addition, on March 28, 1961, the president announced an expansion of the Minuteman I program from 540 to 600 missiles.[31] Finally, a new unified strategic operations plan (SIOP or Single Integrated Operations Program) was adopted to ensure that all aspects of the U.S. strategic strategy were closely integrated and would work together more smoothly in the event of a crisis.[32]

Emphasis on the quantitative buildup of U.S. strategic weapons also occurred the following year as funds for 200 additional Minuteman I missiles were included in the fiscal budget for 1963. In addition, 150 Minuteman IIs and six additional Polaris submarines were included in the 1964 fiscal budget.

A shift toward more emphasis on the qualitative aspects of strategic weapons systems began to occur in 1964, Soviet analysts maintain. McNamara announced that Minuteman Is would be replaced with the more accurate single warhead Minuteman IIs which would make a counterforce strategy more credible. Even more important, a decision was made to deploy multiple reentry vehicles (MRVs) on Polaris A-3 missiles. Although not so dangerous themselves, the MRVs have been seen by Soviet analysts as precursors to MIRVs.[33] This was followed by a decision in 1966 to cancel the Minuteman II program in favor of intensifying work on the Minuteman III which was to be outfitted with a MIRVed system. The qualitative arms race was further intensified in 1967 with the allocation of funds for the development of an ABM system which had as its goal "to damage the opponent's ability to deliver a second strike . . . while creating additional possibilities for the development of a counterforce, i.e., first strike strategy."[34]

By the end of the Democratic administration, the scope of U.S. strategic power had been significantly expanded. The development of a flexible triad of strategic systems—bombers, ICBMs, and SLBMs—had been established. The latter two systems were especially invulnerable to Soviet attack and formed in Soviet eyes a sound basis for the protection of U.S. interests and for the operation of the flexible response doctrine.

1968–1974: The Nixon Administration and Strategic Sufficiency

In contrast to Soviet perceptions, the Republican candidate during the presidential campaign of 1968 insisted that the Democrats had "lost" U.S. strategic superiority vis-à-vis the USSR. But after assuming office, President Nixon and his senior advisors seriously revised their assessment. They came to the conclusion that meaningful strategic nuclear superiority was unattainable. The political problem, however, was to develop a new strategic doctrine that would fall short of unlimited superiority but would go beyond the idea of parity which Nixon had sharply criticized during the election campaign. The result was the development of doctrine of strategic sufficiency.

The Nixon administration adopted four criteria in developing the doctrine of strategic sufficiency. First, the United States must maintain an adequate second strike capability to deter an all-out surprise attack on U.S. strategic forces. Second, U.S. forces should provide no incentive in a crisis for the Soviet Union to strike the United States first. Third, the United States must be able to prevent the Soviet Union from inflicting considerably greater urban and industrial destruction than U.S. forces could inflict on the USSR in a nuclear war. Fourth, the United States should be able to defend itself against small nuclear attacks or accidental launches.[35] Soviet analysts have expressed criticism with regard to all four criteria.

Maintaining an Effective Retaliatory Capability

At least one Soviet analyst considered this criterion little different from the concept of "guaranteed destruction" developed by McNamara.[36] But another senior Soviet specialist claimed that it was a more dangerous concept than the McNamara doctrine. Whereas McNamara provided a mathematical formula to determine when the minimum level of "guaranteed destruction" had been achieved, the criterion of strategic sufficiency was open-ended. This criterion gave U.S. military leadership the "theoretical basis" for excessive reliance on "increases in military strength."[37]

One should note that the Soviets themselves have never provided U.S. policymakers with as clear an indication of strategic sufficiency as did Secretary McNamara. In fact, one might argue that if the Soviets had provided the United States with such a clear statement in the early 1970s then much of the uncertainty associated with Soviet strategic development might have been curtailed. Such uncertainty generated by the Soviet Union is a major factor fueling the strategic arms race.

Crisis Stability

According to Soviet analysts, by attempting to protect U.S. missiles through the development of ABM systems, the United States would have stimulated and did in the end stimulate the development of new offensive systems. These systems, especially MIRVs, have been very destabilizing, for they have involved major advances in modern technology, such as increases in missile accuracy. Furthermore, in a crisis situation this type of destabilization can lead to the perceived need to preempt. The incentive to go for a first strike as a means of avoiding large-scale losses to one's own forces has thereby been increased.[38]

Damage Assessment

By attempting to ensure that more damage is inflicted on the USSR than on the United States in "any type of circumstances of nuclear conflict," Soviet analysts argue that the United States sought to develop new U.S. strategic forces to ensure that Soviet losses will always be greater than those suffered by the United States. Furthermore, U.S. determination to make the USSR suffer more casualties is in reality a prescription for victory in a nuclear war, i.e., the United States seems to believe it can fight and win a nuclear war.[39]

One cannot fail to note that the Soviets have strived throughout the 1960s, 1970s, and 1980s to be precisely in such a situation if possible. Soviet counterforce developments conjoined with conventional force modernization programs reveal a steady Soviet interest in a situation where the Soviet Union could prevail in a global war if such a war appears necessary to the very survival of the Soviet state.

Small-Scale Attacks

This factor, according to a Soviet writer, was aimed at the development of an ABM system. The ABM's purpose is to undermine the ability of a country to deliver a counter blow in the event it is attacked by the United States.[40]

One cannot fail to note that the Soviet ABM deployments permitted under the SALT I accord are precisely to deal with the small-scale attack problem. British, French, and Chinese strategic forces provide a threat against which Soviet ABM forces would be used in contingencies short of U.S.-Soviet central systems exchange.

In short, the doctrine of sufficiency "only minimally tied the hands of the Administration in public in making concrete decisions for the development of weapons systems."[41] In practical terms, it led to "increased military spending."[42] Although Washington viewed strategic sufficiency as a defensive doctrine, to the Soviet Union the doctrine was a prescription for continued strategic modernization. As V. V. Larionov of the USA Institute put it, "What is seen as sufficiency on one side, can be viewed by the other as a drive for superiority."[43] As a consequence, one Soviet analyst noted, the USSR had no choice at this time, but to take the necessary steps to thwart Washington's plans.[44] As one might expect, Soviet analysts recognize the validity of the action-reaction problem from primarily the U.S. side. Soviet strategic force developments are perceived to be legitimate "reactions" to U.S. developments, but are not recognized as legitimate causes in the further development of U.S. programs.

Seen from the Soviet perspective, the efforts by the United States to develop strategic power at this time were primarily centered in two areas, the ABM system and MIRVs. The anti-ballistic system was originally designed to provide a thin shield of protection against China. By 1969, the Soviets argue, the system had been redesigned and retargeted against the USSR.[45]

Despite congressional misgivings over the utility of an ABM system, Nixon went ahead with the program for two reasons, in the Soviet view. Nixon wished to avoid a confrontation with the Pentagon and the "military-industrial complex" over the issue. He also hoped to use the ABM as a "bargaining chip" in negotiations with the Soviet Union. The anti-military mood within the United States nurtured by the Vietnam War as well as congressional concern over both the size of the military budget and the technical practicality of ABM systems, led to a U.S. debate on the ABM that was "the sharpest in the whole history" of the U.S. nuclear program.[46] Throughout the U.S. debate, the administration indicated the need to keep the program as a "trump card" in negotiations with the USSR on limiting strategic weapons.[47]

Soviet interpretations emphasize that for the U.S. military, the MIRV program was a key one designed to develop U.S. strategic power through the qualitative improvement of U.S. strategic forces. Such qualitative development was especially important at a time of increasing numerical equality in launchers.

The development of MIRVs had a major impact on U.S. strategic power. The increased number of warheads obtained through the MIRVing process dramatically increased the range of targets subject to U.S. strategic attack. From the Soviet standpoint, the question became one of determining when the United States would gain a sufficient combination of quantity and accuracy to be able to endanger Soviet land-based systems in a first strike. While a quantitative increase was occurring in MIRVed warheads, a general program of technical modernization of the U.S. strategic force structure (i.e., improving reliability, combat readiness, flexibility, and accuracy) was underway as well.[48]

The Soviet response to the MIRV problem is typical of the Soviet approach of dealing with an adversary from a position of strength. The Soviets evidenced no clear interest in controlling the MIRV process in the Nixon years. This was an area in which the United

States had evidenced a clear technological lead and was an area so significant to the future of strategic power that the Soviets accelerated their own development efforts. Soviet force structure developments combined the traditional large size of Soviet missiles (i.e., large throw-weight) with the new MIRVing capability to create formidable ICBMs in the 1970s such as the SS-18. Thus, while at the outset of the MIRVing process in the 1970s, the Soviets were concerned that the United States might gain the upper hand in being able to threaten Soviet ICBMs, the reverse in fact had become the case by the early 1980s.

From the Soviet standpoint, the SALT I agreements had a contradictory impact on limiting the two threats that most concerned the Soviets in the strategic programs of the Nixon administration, namely, the ABM and MIRV programs. The ABM treaty not only put an end to new types of U.S. systems and to work on a number of technical projects, it also worked as a stabilizing factor. The ABM treaty reduced the chances for either side to carry out a first strike since both sides left themselves open to retaliation from the other side.[49]

The MIRV problem, however, was not resolved by the Interim Agreement which together with the ABM agreement made up SALT I. The Interim Agreement did limit "some aspects of the qualitative modernization of strategic forces."[50] In particular, one Soviet analyst underscored the usefulness of the provisions prohibiting the substitution of light ICBMs developed prior to 1964 for heavy missiles, and the requirement that an equal number of SLBMs and ballistic missile submarines be withdrawn as new ones entered service.[51] Nonetheless, Soviet analysts frequently accused the United States of attempting to take advantage of SALT I by accelerating the MIRVing process. According to Soviet analysts, the 1972 agreements notably failed to limit: the numbers of warheads;[52] qualitative improvements, such as, increases in accuracy, reliability, penetrability, and the development of new systems;[53] U.S. forward-based systems;[54] and long-range aviation.[55]

Soviet analysts argue that the U.S. military-industrial complex redoubled its efforts to gain "one-sided advantages" vis-à-vis the USSR, especially in MIRVing, when SALT I seemed imminent. In order to get Pentagon support, the administration agreed to buildup U.S. military forces, intensify work on the development of technically complex systems, continue modernization of existing systems not limited by SALT I, and, perhaps most importantly, develop new systems not restricted by the treaty.[56] Of particular concern were such systems as the Trident SSBN, the cruise missile, maneuvering reentry vehicles

(MaRV), the neutron warhead, and the MX ICBM in a mobile mode.[57] To this list, another Soviet commentator added the development of the B-1 bomber.[58]

In short, the SALT I agreements restricted the ABM threat to the Soviet Union, but did little to deal with the qualitative development of offensive forces, especially with regard to MIRVs. The Soviets responded to this "threat" by an impressive strategic arms program in the 1970s. The core of this effort was a successful MIRVing program of their own which created a sound basis of deterrence to the United States and which met the U.S. MIRV threat operating outside of SALT I boundaries. The MIRV problem could then be addressed in the SALT II treaty on the basis of increased Soviet strength in this area.

1974–1976: The Ford Administration and Essential Equivalence

Despite its importance as an indicator of Washington's formal acceptance of parity, Soviet analysts underscore that the SALT I agreements were limited in nature. Not only were these agreements accompanied by increased U.S. arms spending, they also led to a call within the United States for the kind of overall equality between the two sides in strategic weapons that the Soviets interpret as a quest for strategic superiority. For example, the Jackson Amendment in 1972 called for equal limits on the quantitative levels of both sides' forces in future arms control agreements without dealing with qualitative competition. This amendment, in turn, had a strong influence on the development of the doctrine of essential equivalence first proposed by Secretary of Defense James Schlesinger in 1973.[59]

The doctrine of essential equivalence worked to U.S. advantage in light of the flexibility of the U.S. strategic triad and against Soviet interests with the heavy reliance by the Soviet Union on land-based missiles. According to Soviet writers, essential equivalence called for the United States to obtain equality in those areas in which the USSR had superiority (e.g., heavy missiles), while at the same time maintaining superiority in those areas in which it already possessed superiority (e.g., accuracy). Furthermore, Soviet analysts note, proponents of essential equivalence maintained that a U.S. president should not be put in a position of having no alternative but to respond to a nuclear attack with the massive use of nuclear weapons. He should have the option of delivering either selective or massive strikes. In essence, this was a call for "limited nuclear war."

Essential equivalence led to an acceleration of U.S. weapons programs that could be used to fight limited nuclear wars. Especially important in this regard were improvements in the accuracy of ICBM and SLBM warheads. U.S. proponents of essential equivalence hoped, according to Soviet analysts, that this doctrine would give the United States a high degree of flexibility in the use of its strategic forces. As long as an attack on the military and industrial targets in the USSR did not destroy large numbers of people, U.S. analysts projected that the Soviets would be restrained by the "strong response potential" of the United States from destroying U.S. cities.[60] Soviet analysts portray the doctrine of essential equivalence as an attempt by the United States to achieve "qualitative superiority in the face of the quantitative restrictions imposed on United States and Soviet strategic forces by Soviet-American agreements."[61]

Soviet analysts have expressed several concerns with the doctrine of essential equivalence. First, with its emphasis on targeting a relatively small number of military targets while holding back the majority of the U.S. nuclear arsenal in reserve, essential equivalence increases the danger of a nuclear war. It raises the possibility of tactical nuclear weapons being utilized without escalation to central systems.[62] In comparison with the McNamara doctrine, for example, "it lowers the escalation threshold of conflicts, by which strategic nuclear weapons may be utilized in a war."[63] Second, because of the emphasis on the need for high degrees of accuracy and on the need to increase the effectiveness of strategic weapons against military targets, the doctrine of essential equivalence has legitimized for the United States the need to develop a new generation of U.S. strategic weapons. Such weapons as the Minuteman III with the Mark 12-A warhead, the MX ICBM, and the Trident submarine with the D-5 warhead are designed as counterforce weapons with a first strike ability.[64] Because the doctrine postulated the need to deliver a second strike in certain contingencies, essential equivalence, unlike the McNamara doctrine, is viewed by Soviet analysts as a call for a second strike doctrine that operates as a second echelon to support a first strike, rather than as a reliable protection against a bolt-from-the-blue attack.[65]

Despite the qualitative buildup in the strategic area, a number of factors in the Soviet view combined to engender prospects for further arms limitations agreements. Such factors included: concern within the United States over the impact that the Schlesinger doctrine and U.S. strategic programs could have on U.S.-Soviet relations; an attempt by newly appointed President Ford to enhance his "popularity and authority" within the United States prior to the 1976 election by reaching a strategic arms control agreement with the Soviets; and the willingness of the USSR to postpone for the future the question of the inclusion of U.S. forward-based systems in strategic arms limitations discussions.[66]

Because of such factors, the Vladivostok Agreement was signed on November 24, 1974. The most important aspect of the accords, from a Soviet standpoint, was the limitation placed on launchers (limited to an overall level of 2,400 with a subtotal of 1,320 MIRVed launchers).[67] For the first time, long-range aviation was also limited.[68]

As is usual with Soviet commentaries on arms control agreements with the United States, the Vladivostok Agreement was viewed as having been seized on by the Pentagon to lobby for increased funds, particularly for air-, sea-, and ground-launched cruise missiles. In addition, at this time, the Pentagon began to intensify its campaign against the Soviet Backfire bomber and an attempt was undertaken within the United States to link foreign policy events outside of Europe with the SALT process. Nevertheless, despite these concerns, on balance, Soviet writers welcomed the Vladivostok Agreement and treated it as a major step forward.[69]

Soviet commentary on the strategic policy of the Ford administration underscores the simultaneous continuation of efforts to reach a SALT II agreement with efforts by the military-industrial complex to build up U.S. strategic forces. In January 1976, for example, the Soviets claimed that then U.S. Secretary of State Henry Kissinger agreed in Moscow to a compromise that called for bombers equipped with strategic cruise missiles to be included in the 1,320 limit on MIRVed launchers. In addition, it was agreed that the development of ground- and sea-launched cruise missiles with a range greater than 600 kilometers would be banned. In returning to Washington, Kissinger told reporters that the SALT II Treaty had been 90 percent agreed.[70] Nonetheless, work was not completed on the SALT II Treaty before the end of the Ford administration. According to one Soviet analyst, this was primarily due to vacillation on the part of President Ford and opposition by the military-industrial complex to the treaty.[71]

The Ford administration also continued efforts to strengthen U.S. strategic power. The Schlesinger doctrine placed emphasis on plans to conduct selective counterforce strikes against military targets. As a result, work was intensified on increasing the accuracy of ICBM and SLBM warheads.[72]

It should be noted that Soviet strategic development in the 1970s had precisely the goal of creating a significant counterforce capability against U.S. ICBMs. Soviet concern over the probable development by the United States in the 1970s and 1980s of a counterforce capability was founded upon the desire to maintain a Soviet edge in this area.

The Soviets put the United States in a very difficult bind. If the United States threatens Soviet ICBMs, then the United States undermines Soviet deterrence. But if the United States does not in some way deal with the Soviet counterforce threat, then the United States is put at greater degrees of risk than are acceptable.

1976–1980: The Carter Administration

Under the Carter administration, U.S. strategic policy was contradictory. On the one hand, the B-1 and MX programs were cancelled or slowed down, military spending was reduced, and interest in strategic arms limitation agreements was reaffirmed.[73] On the other hand, the United States allocated funds for air-launched cruise missiles, induced NATO to increase military spending and to agree to deploy long-range theater nuclear forces, decided to go ahead with plans for deploying neutron warheads, tested the Tomahawk cruise missile, and began equipping the Minuteman III missile with the Mk-12A warhead.[74]

Meanwhile, discussions with the USSR over the SALT II Treaty continued. The talks had an inauspicious start when the United States put forth a proposal aimed at "revising" the Vladivostok accords by means of the so-called Comprehensive Proposal for deep cuts. According to Soviet analysts, this proposal, which Secretary of Defense Cyrus Vance presented in Moscow in March 1977, would have reduced the overall number of launchers on both sides to the 1,800–2,000 range, those with MIRVed warheads to 1,100. This proposal would have required a radical restructuring of Soviet strategic forces away from "heavy" ICBMs.

Soviet analysts strongly condemned this proposal on several grounds. The proposal did not limit U.S. forward-based systems (FBS) in Europe, which would have assumed an even greater role in the U.S. strategic arsenal if the overall level of strategic systems were dramatically reduced.[75] The proposal did not limit the U.S. systems that most concerned the Soviets. The United States had a clear lead in a number of areas of strategic modernization, such as the Trident missile and submarine systems and the Mk-12A warhead. In fact, Soviet analysts note, the Carter administration's "real" intentions became clear two months later when Washington announced its plans to go ahead with outfitting the Minuteman III with the Mk-12A warhead.[76] For these and other reasons, Moscow firmly rejected the proposal. As Foreign Minister Andrei Gromyko put it, "After an objective look at these proposals, it is not difficult to conclude that they are aimed at achieving a one-sided advantage for the United States to the disadvantage of the Soviet Union, its security, and the security of our allies and friends."[77]

All in all, one Soviet writer argued, the Carter administration's strategic arms program together with its early approach to the SALT II talks were an attempt to achieve three major goals:

> First, to achieve the possibility of maintaining nuclear weapons as an active instrument of policy, including the possibility of their real utilization. . . . Second, to achieve again the future superiority over the Soviet Union (this goal is clearly reflected in the course of the United States's speeding-up of the arms race and the attempt to achieve military-technical superiority). Third, while continuing to count on a nuclear struggle with the Soviet Union, the Carter Administration sought to ensure "strategic stability" by means of agreements with the Soviet Union on specific limitations and reductions of strategic forces, which in the American view, lowered the risk of a surprise attack on the United States and do not undermine the basis of its nuclear power.[78]

The Soviet rebuff in March 1977, together with increasing difficulties for Washington around the world (the Middle East, Iran, Nicaragua, and Chinese "aggression" in Indo-China), forced the Carter administration, in the Soviet view, to reevaluate its approach to the SALT negotiations.[79] The United States became more reasonable in its negotiating stance. The result was the SALT II agreement signed by Carter and Brezhnev in Vienna on June 18, 1979.

In the Soviet view, the SALT II Treaty had a number of positive effects in controlling U.S. strategic programs. Limits were placed on the following systems: on the number of cruise missiles that could be deployed; on the speed with which Trident submarines could be deployed; and on the development of new mobile land-based ICBMs. In addition, the development of mobile land- and sea-based cruise missiles was postponed.[80]

But negative trends in the United States were reducing the chances that the United States would implement the SALT II accord. In the view of Soviet analysts, U.S. foreign policy failures, an aggravation of internal economic and social problems, and nostalgia on the part of the U.S. populace for the days of global predominance increased the significance of the right-wing within U.S. "ruling circles." In an effort to demonstrate its firmness in foreign policy and to placate the right-wing within the country, the Carter administration began to rely more heavily on "anti-Sovietism" in its foreign policy. On the internal front, the primary result was a strengthening of the military-industrial complex. Eventually, the Soviets claim, this led the Carter administration to postpone the ratification of the SALT II Treaty.[81]

In addition to concerns over the fate of SALT II, Soviet analysts expressed concern regarding the direction of strategic doctrinal development under Carter. The Carter administration had developed a new "countervailing strategy."

This strategy (embodied in Presidential Directive 59, i.e., PD-59) has been sharply criticized by Soviet analysts on four grounds. First, the new strategy relied upon the use of limited nuclear strikes against a large number of targets, including political and military control centers. Unlike the Schlesinger doctrine which aimed to terminate a war by demonstrating resolve to the enemy through the use of individual selective strikes, the new strategy aimed at the broader goal of militarily paralyzing one's opponent and thereby hoping to force him to capitulate. Second, the new strategy legitimized the deployment of new U.S. medium-range missiles in Western Europe. Third, the new strategy emphasized the need to be prepared to fight a protracted nuclear war. Fourth, the strategy required an ability to execute a disarming first strike capability. Washington hoped to use its increasingly sophisticated guidance and targeting systems to destroy the USSR's main military might and to thereby destroy Moscow's ability to retaliate in a wartime setting.[82]

The new strategy represented another attempt by the United States to develop its strategic power through reliance upon the qualitative development of its nuclear forces. As one Soviet writer put it: "Its essence is to ensure superiority for the United States in nuclear forces so that after an exchange of "counterforce" strikes, the United States will retain a superior capability to destroy the population and industrial centers and be able to restrain the other side from delivering a retaliatory strike."[83]

U.S. efforts to implement the new strategy, according to a Soviet analyst, focused upon the development of mobile ICBMs, Trident missiles, ALCM-equipped B-52s, and the Pershing II ground-launched cruise missile (GLCM). The United States has been working particularly hard to improve the accuracy and yield of these weapons as well as to reduce U.S. vulnerability while continuing to improve the survivability of U.S. command, control, and communications facilities.[84]

By the end of the Carter administration, Soviet writers while refusing to call the SALT II Treaty dead expressed sharp concern over developments within the United States. The promulgation of the new countervailing strategy, the U.S. failure to ratify the SALT II Treaty, and Washington's continuing push toward the development of increasingly more sophisticated technical systems were viewed as particularly threatening to Soviet interests.[85]

1980–1984: The Reagan Administration

While the Reagan administration accepted the basic outlines of the Carter administration's strategic programs, it has significantly expanded on them, according to Soviet analysts. Increased funds have been allocated to four major areas: the fast-reaction force, conventional forces, intercontinental nuclear forces, and theater nuclear forces. In addition, a special effort has been made to try to achieve military superiority by relying on U.S. technological advantages.[86]

The idea that the United States has been moving toward improved counterforce and therefore enhanced first strike capability is a constant theme in recent Soviet writings. One analyst writing in mid-1983 argued that the decision to deploy the Pershing II and cruise missiles, the MX ICBM, and the Trident D-5 SLBM is aimed at giving the United States a first strike capability.[87] Also upsetting to the Soviets has been President Reagan's decision to develop anti-missile defense weapons that might be deployed in space. The development of such systems would "significantly increase the danger that tragically mistaken decisions could be taken during crisis situations."[88]

To create public support for the development of new U.S. strategic systems, Soviet specialists charge that the Reagan administration has tried to make the idea of nuclear war more acceptable. The Reagan administration has worked out a number of scenarios for limited nuclear war. The Reagan administration is not only talking about deterrence of nuclear war, "but of the readiness of the U.S. to actually engage in it."[89] As a senior Soviet military analyst put it:

> The United States has once again proved unable to resist the temptation to utilize its technical achievements in order to improve its counterforce potential and further improve its C^3 systems. In this regard, the Reagan Administration has gone even further; it is actively implementing the principles set forth in NSDM-242 and PD-59. Considering that many people in the new administration base their nuclear strategy on the possibility of a "limited" nuclear war, it should be noted that this fact is fraught with extreme danger. Directives like PD-59 give the Secretary of Defense and the Joint Chiefs of Staff a foundation for convincing the country's political leadership of the possibility of military victory in a nuclear war.[90]

Thus, by the beginning of the 1980s, Soviet leaders perceived an acceleration of the U.S. threat, a threat of long-standing concern. As Marshal Ogarkov stated in 1982: "Even a quick analysis of the evolution of American strategic doctrine shows that it always has had as the basis of its content the idea of nuclear war against the USSR and possesses a clearly expressed aggressive character."[91]

In conclusion, two basic qualities of the Soviet commentary on the development of U.S. strategic policy should be noted. First, public Soviet commentary on strategic arms developments focuses on the pattern of U.S. "stimulus" and Soviet "response." Significant Soviet contributions to this race tend to be equated simply with the "modernization" of weapons rather than with the escalation of the arms race. Second, this quality of commentary by Soviet policy analysts tends to reflect a broader reluctance by Soviet policymakers to recognize publicly the nature of what constitutes legitimate U.S. interests in the strategic arms modernization process.

In spite of these two major reservations concerning the nature of Soviet analyses, Soviet commentary does reveal two significant expressions of concern about the nature of the U.S. strategic challenge. First, Soviets note with admiration the inventiveness of U.S. strategic force structure development. The United States has clearly been seen as a dynamic actor in shaping the nature of contemporary warfare. Second, the Soviets especially emphasize the high quality of U.S. scientific and technological capabilities. These capabilities are perceived to be a major force generating the continued U.S. ability to develop strategic power.

In short, the Soviets see a continued strong commitment by the United States to the development of its strategic power, which tends to undermine strategic stability. The strategic balance is at best a dynamic equilibrium; U.S. technological developments create strategic uncertainties that require a Soviet response. Given the commitment of both sides not to fall significantly behind in the strategic arms race, parity tends to be reestablished at a higher armaments level and at great cost to both sides.

Notes

1. V. V. Zhurkin et al., "Posledstviia vliianiia nauchno-tekhnicheskoi revoliutsii na voennuiu politiku SShA," in Georgy Arbatov, ed., SShA Nauchno-tekhnicheskaia revoliutsiia i tendentsii vneshnei politiki (Moscow: Mezhdunarodnye otnosheniia, 1974), p. 45. For a comprehensive treatment of Soviet perceptions of the U.S. military-technological challenge, see Erik Hoffmann and Robbin Laird, "The Scientific-Technological Revolution" and Soviet Foreign Policy (Elmsford, New York: Pergamon Press, 1982), Chapter 4.

2. V. M. Kulish, ed., Voennaia sila i mezhdunarodnye otnosheniia (Moscow: Mezhdunarodnye otnosheniia, 1972), p. 222.

3. Ibid., p. 226.

4. Ibid.

5. Zhurkin et al., "Posledstviia vliianiia," p. 45.

6. K. V. Spirov, "The Effects of Scientific-Technical Progress on the Military Doctrines and Armed Forces of Imperialism," in Col. Gen. N. A. Lomov, ed., *The Revolution in Military Affairs*, trans. by the U.S. Air Force (Washington, D.C.: Government Printing Office, n.d.), p. 252.

7. V. V. Borisov, *Opasnaia stavka: Nauchno-tekhnicheskaia revoliutsiia i voennye prigotovleniia SShA* (Moscow: Voenizdat, 1979), p. 21.

8. G. A. Trofimenko, *SShA: Politika, voina, ideologiia* (Moscow: Mysl', 1976), p. 163.

9. A. A. Roshchin, *Mezhdunarodnaia bezopasnost' i iadernoe oruzhie* (Moscow: Mezhdunarodnye otnosheniia, 1980), p. 98.

10. V. M. Mil'shtein, *Voenno-promyshlennyi kompleks i vneshniaia politika SShA* (Moscow: Mezhdunarodnye otnosheniia, 1975), p. 144.

11. Ibid.

12. Iu. V. Katasonov, "Politika, ekonomika i voenno-strategicheskie kontseptsiia," in R. G. Bogdanov et al., eds., *SShA: Voenno-strategicheskie kontseptsii* (Moscow: Nauka, 1980), p. 22.

13. V. V. Zhurkin, "Respublikanskaia administratsiia: Formirovanie voenno-politicheskoi strategii," *SShA* 5 (1982), p. 10.

14. A. Arbatov, *Bezopasnost' v iadernyi vek i politika Vashingtona* (Moscow: Politizdat, 1980), p. 71.

15. V. Larionov, "Razvitie sredstv vooruzheniia i strategicheskie kontseptsii SShA," *Mirovaia ekonomika i mezhdunarodnoe otnosheniia* 6 (1966), p. 75.

16. Iu. V. Katasonov, "Voennaia doktrina i voenno-strategicheskie kontseptsii," in Bogdanov et al., eds., *SShA: Voenno-strategicheskie kontseptsii*, p. 50.

17. Ibid., pp. 50–51.

18. Trofimenko, *SShA: Politika, voina, ideologiia*, p. 215.

19. Lawrence Freedman, *The Evolution of Nuclear Strategy* (London: Macmillan, 1981), pp. 232–233.

20. Trofimenko, *SShA: Politika, voina, ideologiia*, p. 230.

21. Zhurkin et al., "Posledstviia vliianiia," p. 52.

22. Trofimenko, *SShA: Politika, voina, ideologiia*, p. 231.

23. M. Mil'shtein, "Amerikanskie voennye doktriny: preemstvennost' i modifikatsiia," *Mirovaia ekonomika i mezhdunarodnye otnosheniia* 7 (1971), p. 31.

24. Zhurkin et al., "Posledstviia vliianiia," p. 46, and L. V. Semeiko, "Strategischeskia iadernaia voina," in Bogdanov et al., eds., *SShA: Voenno-strategicheskie kontseptsii*, p. 188.

25. M. Mil'shtein, "O nekotorykh voenno-strategicheskikh kontseptsiiakh amerikanskogo imperializma," *Mirovaia ekonomika i mezhdunarodnye otnosheniia* 8 (1962), p. 90.

26. Trofimenko, *SShA: Politika, voina, ideologiia*, p. 241.

27. Ibid., pp. 242–243.

28. Ibid.

29. Arbatov, *Bezopasnost'*, p. 18, and Semeiko, "Strategicheskaia iadernaia voina," p. 184.

30. Arbatov, *Bezopasnost'*, p. 28 and Trofimenko, *SShA: Politika, voina, ideologiia*, p. 242.

31. Arbatov, *Bezopasnost'*, p. 26.

32. Ibid., p. 28.

33. Ibid., p. 48.

34. Trofimenko, *SShA: Politika, voina, ideologiia*, p. 253. See also, Arbatov, *Bezopasnost'*, p. 50.

35. As summarized in Jerome H. Kahan, *Security in the Nuclear Age* (Washington, D.C.: The Brookings Institution, 1975), p. 149. Semeiko's listing of the four criteria are an exact translation of Kahan's although he cites Laird's original statement. A. Arbatov is slightly different, but agrees on all major points.

36. Arbatov, *Bezopasnost'*, p. 117.

37. L. V. Semeiko, "Stroitel'stvo strategicheskikh iadernykh sil," in Bogdanov et al., eds., *SShA: Voenno-strategicheskie kontseptsii*, pp. 153–155.

38. Ibid., pp. 155–156. See also, Arbatov, *Bezopasnost'*, p. 117.

39. Ibid.

40. Semeiko, "Stroitel'stvo strategicheskikh iadernykh sil," pp. 157–158.

41. Arbatov, *Bezopasnost'*, p. 118. See also, O. Bykov, "O nekotorykh chertakh vneshnepoliticheskoi strategii SShA," *Mirovaia ekonomika i mezhdunarodnye otnosheniia* 4 (1971), p. 57, and G. I. Sviatov, "Politika SShA v oblasti vooruzhenii v 70-e gody," in *Amerikanskii ezhegodnik 1980* (Moscow: Nauka, 1981), p. 168.

42. N. S. Solobovnik, "Izmeneniia voennoi politiki i voennoi doktriny SShA v kontse 60-nachale 70-kh godov," in Kulish, ed., *Voennaia sila*, p. 81.

43. V. V. Larionov, "Strategicheskie debaty," *SShA* 3 (1970), p. 19. See also, M. Mil'shtein, "Amerikanskie voennye doktriny: preemstvennost' i modifikatsiia," p. 32.

44. Arbatov, *Bezopasnost'*, p. 188. Arbatov fails to provide any clues as to what these steps are.

45. Ibid., p. 118.

46. Ibid., pp. 119–120.

47. Ibid., p. 124.

48. Ibid., pp. 134–138.

49. Ibid., p. 143.

50. Ibid.

51. Ibid.

52. G. A. Arbatov et al., *Global'naia strategiia SShA v usloviiakh nauchno-tekhnicheskoi revoliutsii* (Moscow: Mysl', 1979), p. 23.

53. Ibid. See also, M. A. Mil'shtein, "Progress na glavnom napravlenii," *SShA* 2 (1975), p. 6.

54. Arbatov et al., *Global'naia strategiia*, pp. 23–24.

55. M. A. Mil'shtein and L. S. Semeiko, "Ogranichenie strategicheskikh vooruzhenii: problemy i perspektivy," *SShA* 12 (1973), p. 3.

56. Arbatov, *Bezopasnost'*, pp. 157–180.

57. Ibid.

58. Sviatov, "Politika SShA," p. 177.

59. Semeiko, "Stroitel'stvo strategicheskikh iadernykh sil," p. 161.

60. Arbatov, *Bezopasnost'*, p. 193.

61. Trofimenko, *SShA: Politika, voina, ideologiia*, p. 208.

62. Sviatov, "Politika SShA," p. 184.

63. Ibid., p. 187.

64. Ibid., pp. 184, 196. See also Trofimenko, *SShA: Politika, voina, ideologiia*, p. 316.

65. Arbatov, *Bezopasnost'*, p. 192.

66. Ibid., pp. 219–222.

67. Ibid., p. 332.

68. Mil'shtein, "Progress na glavnom napravlenii," p. 9.

69. See, for example, "Vladivostokskaia vstrecha," *SShA* 12 (1974), pp. 3–5.

70. Arbatov, *Bezopasnost'*, p. 235.

71. Ibid., p. 235.

72. Sviatov, "Politika SShA," pp. 186–187.

73. Ibid., p. 188.

74. Arbatov, *Bezopasnost'*, p. 249. See also, Iu. V. Katasonov, "Mekhanizm formirovaniia voenno-politicheskoi i voennoi strategii SShA," in Bogdanov et al., eds., *SShA: Voenno-strategicheskie kontseptsii*, p. 122.

75. Arbatov, *Bezopasnost'*, p. 255.

76. N. M. Nikol'skii and A. V. Grishin, *Nauchno-tekhnicheskii progress: Mezhdunarodnye otnosheniia* (Moscow: Mezhdunarodnye otnosheniia, 1978), p. 144.

77. *Pravda*, April 1, 1977.

78. Katasonov, "Mekhanizm formirovaniia voenno-politicheskoi i voennoi strategii SShA," p. 122.

79. Arbatov, *Bezopasnost'*, p. 256.

80. Ibid., p. 263.

81. A. G. Arbatov, "Strategicheskii paritet i politika administratsii Kartera," *SShA* 11 (1980), p. 33. See also, Iu. V. Katasonov, "Voenno-politicheskaia strategiia SShA na rubezhe 70-80kh godov," *SShA* 2 (1980), p. 10.

82. R. G. Bogdanov, "Ogranichenie i sokrashchenie strategicheskikh vooruzhenii serdtsevina mezhdunarodnoi bezopasnosti, problema chrezvychainaia," *SShA* 5, (1981), p. 5.

83. G. A. Trofimenko, "Vashington: Kurs na napriazhennost," *SShA* 6 (1980), p. 11.

84. Ibid. See also Bogdanov, "Ogranichenie i sokrashchenie," p. 113, and Katasonov, "Voenno-politicheskaia strategiia SShA na rubezhe 70-80kh godov," p. 21.

85. L. Semeiko, "Directive 59: Development or Leap?" *Novoe Vremia* 38 (September 19, 1980), pp. 5–7, trans. in *Joint Publications Research Service*, 191, September 30, 1980; V. Zhurkin, "In Pursuit of the Impossible Goal: The New U.S. Nuclear Strategy," *Literaturnaia gazeta*, September 17, 1980, p. 14; trans. in *Joint Publications Research Service*, 185, September 22, 1980.

86. G. A. Trofimenko, "Osnovnye postulaty vneshnei politiki SShA i sud'by razriadki," *SShA* 7 (1981), p. 14.

87. V. V. Zhurkin, "Kto podryvaet stabil'nost'," *SShA* 7 (1983), pp. 4–5.

88. Ibid., p. 5.

89. V. P. Abarenkov, "SShA i ogranichenie vooruzhenii," *SShA* 10 (1982), p. 8.

90. R. G. Bogdanov, *SShA: Voennaia mashinai politika* (Moscow: Nauka, 1983), pp. 177–178.

91. N. Ogarkov, *Vsegda v gotovnosti k zashchite Otechestva* (Moscow: Voenizdat, 1982), p. 17.

Arms Control and the Soviet Approach to Strategic Parity

The Soviet Approach to SALT I

The SALT I agreements were forged in the period from 1969 to 1972. The centerpiece of the agreement was the Anti-Ballistic Missile Treaty, which remains the most significant limitation on U.S. and Soviet weapons to date. This treaty limited each side to two ABM "deployment areas" of 100 launchers each. This ceiling of 200 launchers was reduced further by a July 1974 protocol to the treaty. By the terms of the 1974 agreement, each side was limited to a single deployment site, with each side free to choose whether to defend an ICBM silo complex or its national capital. In addition to quantitative limits, the ABM treaty placed qualitative restrictions on ABM systems as well, especially with regard to the nature of radar systems that could support ABM missiles. The treaty also included a ban on developing mobile ABM systems and multiple warhead ABM launchers, and prohibitions preventing the upgrading of air defenses into anti-ballistic missiles.

An additional element of SALT I was the Interim Agreement on strategic offensive weapons. Unlike the ABM treaty, which was of unlimited duration, the Interim Agreement was only intended to be binding for five years, although it was informally extended in 1977. The Interim Agreement simply provided for a quantitative freeze on the numbers of deployed strategic systems (ICBMs and SLBMs only). The Interim Agreement did *not* include U.S. and Soviet heavy bombers (which favored U.S. interests). There were no controls set on the numbers of warheads, which was of considerable significance given that the United States was deploying a MIRV system on both its SLBMs and ICBMs and that the Soviets were planning to do so.

Moscow's decision to begin the SALT process in 1969 was made in the context of an ongoing Soviet strategic buildup that was rapidly reducing the quantitative gap between U.S. and Soviet strategic forces. By 1968, the Soviets had deployed 850 ICBMs, and in late 1969 or early 1970 the Soviet land-based missile force surpassed the U.S. arsenal in number of launchers, although not in weapons. Although there was satisfaction with the numerical strategic balance in Moscow, there were also growing anxieties regarding the qualitative competition. Technological advances such as the MIRV and ABM programs underway in the United States in the late 1960s were viewed in Moscow with concern. MIRVs threatened not only to undercut the recent numerical gains by the Soviets in the strategic competition but to decrease the viability of the Soviet arsenal. In addition, Moscow's ABM program was encountering technical difficulties by the late 1960s, and the Soviets were less confident than in the mid-1960s of the capabilities of ABM systems to protect against massive attacks by strategic offensive forces.

In addition to such immediate military concerns, political considerations entered into Moscow's decision to begin SALT. A new round in the arms race would exacerbate East-West relations at a time when the Soviets wanted to promote East-West détente. For example, Moscow was engaged in a diplomatic campaign to secure the application of the Non-Proliferation Treaty to Germany, a matter of great concern to Soviet understanding of the military threat, i.e., the desire for a nonnuclear Germany.

Although political as well as purely military motivations appear to underlie Soviet interest in SALT, the Soviet approach to the SALT I negotiations focused on an effort to impose the maximum restrictions on those U.S. programs judged most threatening by Moscow. In particular, the Soviet Union wished to limit the U.S. ABM and MIRV deployments and to thereby improve its position in the overall strategic balance. Moscow also hoped that negotiations would reduce pressure for new arms deployments in the United States and, furthermore, permit maximum flexibility for Soviet weapons programs. The Soviet leaders, in other words, approached SALT I as an opportunity to bargain about strategic parity in a manner most favorable to their arms modernization programs.

In the very first negotiating session of SALT I (November–December 1969), the Soviet negotiators indicated interest in controlling ABM systems. The Soviet position was that widespread deployment of ABMs would create "suspicions that a first strike was being prepared. . . . A nation, believing that its population was adequately protected, might be less concerned about nuclear war than if it believed such war would be a total disaster."[1] Even at this early stage, the Soviet negotiators indicated a preference for limiting ABMs to a light deployment that would permit them to keep intact their system around Moscow. Soviet concern for a light deployment as opposed to a complete ban was generated in part by concern over the third country nuclear issue, namely, the ability of China, France, or England to attack Moscow with nuclear weapons.

In this initial session, the United States insisted that any ABM agreement include restraints on anti-aircraft missiles and radars. Especially significant to the United States was the need to guard against a Soviet ability to upgrade surface-to-air missile systems to perform as ABM systems. In light of the Soviet Union's air defense system, the United States wished to protect itself against the ABM breakout by means of the upgrading of this air defense system.

These two positions, namely the Soviet desire for thin deployments and the U.S. desire for protection against SAM upgrades, formed the boundaries of the negotiating process surrounding ABMs in SALT I. The eventual agreement provided for the opportunity for very thin deployments. It also provided stringent restrictions on Soviet radar deployments, for the United States argued that it was the quality of the radar system, especially phased array radars, that would allow ABM missiles to strike ballistic missile vehicles in flight. The Soviets did, in fact, accept the U.S. argument and accepted radar restrictions. (The United States began in late 1983 to express public concern that the Soviets might be violating the agreement on radar restrictions.)

The Soviet motivation for negotiating the ABM treaty was generated in part by concern with stopping U.S. deployments of the Safeguard ABM system. According to Gerard Smith, head of the U.S. delegation at SALT I,

> For all its deficiencies, political as well as technical, the United States ABM program had the Soviets worried. This system had missions to defend Minuteman ICBMs, to blunt a low-level Chinese attack, and to destroy warheads from any accidental missile firing. But the Soviets must also have perceived its potential for becoming the basis for a nationwide defense system able to blunt Soviet retaliatory strikes if the Americans struck first. Semenov [the chief Soviet negotiator] observed that, if one side employed ABMs to defend its strategic offensive weapons as well as other "targets" a considerable distance away, would not the other side feel uncertainty that such a thin ABM system could evolve into a system useful to support a first strike strategy? A Soviet later said that a nationwide deployment, even if designed only to protect against a third-country attack or against "light" attacks, could not be considered limited. Their military experts had concluded that a nationwide deployment such as contemplated under the full American program [twelve sites] could too easily be converted into a "heavy"

defense. The Soviets probably were impressed by the fact that the United States development program was making good technical progress. Of twenty-six test firings in 1969 (which the Soviets undoubtedly monitored), eighteen were totally successful, four partially successful, and only four were failures. The Soviet views on ABM levels were much more specific than other Soviet positions. Their comments on the United States ABM program gave a clear indication that limiting ABMs was a primary Soviet aim.[2]

The Soviets were especially concerned that deployments of MIRVs along with ABMs would give the United States a genuine first-strike potential.

Other motivations are more opaque. It would seem that the Soviets had reached a judgment that the primitive state of the art of ballistic missile defense technology simply did not justify the deployment of the 5,000 to 9,000 ABM missile launchers the United States expected the Soviets to deploy.[3] In addition, the ABM decision probably reflected the Soviet judgment that assured destruction was the likely outcome of an all-out nuclear exchange with the United States.

In contrast to their serious interest in ABM controls, the Soviets were much less interested in a limitation of MIRV deployments. The United States proposed to ban the deployment of MIRVs, but the United States, with its MIRVs already fully tested, would be able to produce them much more quickly in case of necessity. The United States also added a wide-ranging on-site inspection requirement for Soviet anti-aircraft missile sites. The Soviets countered with a MIRV production and deployment ban that would have allowed the Soviet Union to test MIRVs. This Soviet proposal was rejected because it was virtually unverifiable.[4]

The Soviet lack of interest in exploring the idea of a MIRV ban was due primarily to the significant technological lead the United States had developed in this area. The U.S. proposal made in 1970 to ban the deployment of MIRVs came less than two months before the United States began deploying them on Minuteman IIIs. In contrast, the Soviets had not even begun to test MIRVs. From a Soviet standpoint, the U.S. ban on testing MIRVs would have frozen the U.S. lead in a critical technology, permitting the United States to "break out" toward strategic superiority if the SALT agreements collapsed. It is very difficult to reach an arms control agreement when the Soviets or the Americans are fearful of being "frozen out" of a strategically significant technology.

The Soviets may have also calculated that the U.S. Minuteman III ICBM and Poseidon SLBM programs made it clear that the United

States was going to counter Soviet numerical superiority in launchers with superiority in numbers of warheads. They may have further calculated that the MIRV genie was out of the bottle. In fact, their resistance to U.S. efforts to limit the numbers of deployed heavy missiles or to define carefully the dimensions of a heavy missile are explained in part by the desire to develop a MIRV option. The Soviets were clearly dedicated in the SALT I negotiations to protect their heavy missile (SS-18 and SS-19) deployment options.

The ABM and MIRV experiences in SALT I provide some indication of how the Soviets conceive of the relationship between arms modernization and arms control. In the ABM case, the Soviets had been sobered in part by the significant technological challenge of creating a truly effective ABM system. Even though U.S. ABM technology was probably perceived to be more advanced than Soviet technology, the Soviets appeared to believe that offensive weapons would have the capability to saturate and defeat ABM systems for a long time to come. An offensive arms race to ensure saturation of relatively ineffective ABM systems was costly and senseless. Hence, banning ABM deployments was possible because the Soviets did *not* fear a rapid break-out capability by the United States in the ABM area if an agreement broke down. An ABM ban also facilitated the modernization of strategic offensive forces by reducing the technological risks confronting new strategic systems.

In contrast, a ban on testing MIRVs would have left the United States in a technologically superior position. Soviet strategic arms modernization would have been impeded by such a ban, not encouraged as in the ABM case. *The Soviet approach to strategic parity accepts the inevitability of technological modernization, but accepts limits to technological development only when Soviet interests are not jeopardized by those deployments.* But the technological challenge must have a roughly symmetrical threat to both Soviet and U.S. interests for the Soviets to accept arms limitations. In the ABM case, neither the United States nor the Soviet Union seemed close to deploying a system so advanced as to confer even short-term strategic advantage in an all-out ABM competition.

From a technological point of view, the impact of the SALT I accords was to increase dramatically the weight of offensive systems in the strategic postures of both superpowers. The Interim Agreement provided only very limited control over offensive systems. According to Wolfe,

> The latitude remaining on both sides for missile modernization, including MIRV, and for a further SLBM buildup on the Soviet side, meant that the net effect of the SALT I agreements was to weight the officially

sanctioned strategic balance even more heavily toward offensive capabilities than had been the case before, suggesting in turn that any new SALT agreements would tend to rest primarily on the conception of balancing off strategic offensive forces against each other.[5]

The Soviets were concerned to provide themselves with as much flexibility as possible to modernize their strategic offensive forces. The SALT I accords ratified a numerical superiority in Soviet ICBM and SLBM launchers but did not include controls for strategic bombers or for numbers of warheads, both areas where the United States had substantial leads. In addition, SALT I did not involve restrictions on intermediate range nuclear systems.

A major political purpose of the SALT negotiations from the Soviet standpoint was to gain recognition of equality with the United States in the strategic competition. The Soviets hoped a recognition that they had attained strategic equality with the United States would lead the United States to recognize "the Soviet 'right,' as a fellow super-power, to receive redress for strategic asymmetries favoring the United States, and to shorten through negotiations the time required to catch up with the United States by unilateral effort alone."[6]

The Soviets hoped that the political commitment of the United States to strategic parity would preclude any U.S. attempt to regain superiority. By signing the SALT I accords, the United States was publicly accepting strategic parity with the Soviet Union. As an *Izvestiia* article published in August 1972 noted, "The documents on strategic arms limitation signed by the President of the United States can appropriately be regarded as official recognition of the fact that relations with the Soviet Union can only be built on the basis of full equality in guaranteeing the security [of each side] and the inadmissibility of a one-sided military superiority."[7]

A further political dimension of the Soviet approach to strategic parity involves Soviet understanding of "equal security." From the Soviet standpoint "genuine" strategic parity would involve "balancing" Soviet nuclear forces with *all* U.S. weapons systems capable of striking Soviet territory (whether deployed in Europe, Asia, or the United States) and all French and British forces which are also capable of threatening Soviet territory. Throughout the negotiations in SALT I, the Soviets insisted on counting U.S. forward-based systems in any agreement governing strategic offensive arms. According to Smith, the U.S. delegation at the SALT I talks heard more about the FBS issue from the Soviet delegation than on any other issue. Smith summarized the Soviet position presented in the SALT I talks as follows:

Agreements on the basis of equal security . . . had to deal with threats as perceived by each side. All nuclear delivery systems which could be used to hit targets in the other country should be covered in SALT, regardless of whether their owners called them strategic or tactical. A Soviet city could just as well be bombed by United States fighter bombers based in Europe or on aircraft carriers as by an ICBM launched from the United States. (A Soviet general told of being bombed while lying wounded in a hospital during the war. It had given him no comfort that the bomb had been dropped by a fighter bomber rather than a heavy bomber.) This principle should define which weapons systems were strategic and to be limited. Weapons systems that could not hit targets in the other country should not be included. Thus, the 600 Soviet MR/IRBMs trained on Western Europe should not be included.[8]

The United States consistently rejected the Soviet FBS concept, proposing instead that the negotiations focus upon "central" systems located in each superpower's territory capable of striking the other's territory. In fact, the Interim Agreement did cover only central systems (although excluding bombers).

Nonetheless, two dimensions of the SALT I process call into question whether the Soviets had jettisoned their concept of strategic parity (equal security) for the U.S. concept (central systems balance). First, the Interim Agreement reflected FBS considerations. As Smith described it,

> The architect of this freeze, Kissinger, justified the Soviet advantage in numbers of missile launchers in part by pointing to the United States advantage in FBS. In briefing congressional leaders on the SALT agreements, Kissinger recalled, "It was decided to exclude from the freeze bombers and so-called forward-based systems. To exclude, that is, the weapons in which this country holds an advantage. . . . We urge the Congress to keep this fact in mind when assessing the numerical ratios of weapons which are subject to the offensive freeze."[9]

Second, the Soviets issued a significant unilateral statement after having agreed to an offensive arms freeze. On May 17, 1972, the Soviet arms delegation issued the following statement which said in part:

> Taking into account that modern ballistic missile submarines are presently in the possession of not only the United States, but also of its NATO allies, the Soviet Union agrees that for the period of effectiveness of the Interim "Freeze" Agreement the United States and its NATO allies have up to 50 such submarines with a total of up to 800 ballistic missile launchers thereon (including 41 United States submarines with 656

ballistic missile launchers). However, if during the period of effectiveness of the Agreement United States allies in NATO should increase the number of their modern submarines to exceed the number of submarines they would have operational or under construction on the date of signature of the Agreement, the Soviet Union will have the right to a corresponding increase in the number of its submarines.[10]

The United States completely rejected this Soviet argument and issued a unilateral statement of its own making clear it did so. Nonetheless, the marker had been laid down by Moscow on the intermediate nuclear weapons issue.

The Soviet Approach to SALT II

The process of negotiating the SALT II agreement took seven years (1972–1979) and spanned three U.S. administrations (Nixon, Ford, and Carter). The first phase of the SALT process was concluded when Ford and Brezhnev signed the Vladivostok Agreement in 1974. The key features of the accord were a ceiling of 2,400 for total offensive strategic nuclear launch vehicles and a subceiling of 1,320 launchers of systems with multiple warheads.

Compared with the SALT I Interim Agreement, the Vladivostok accord introduced two important changes into the SALT framework. First, the Soviets agreed to give up the numerical advantage in launchers they had enjoyed under the Interim Agreement. In return, the accord included heavy bombers in the aggregate ceiling of 2,400 strategic launchers. Heavy bombers had not been included in the Interim Agreement. Second, MIRVs were limited for the first time, albeit at a very high level (1,320 warheads). The ceiling was high enough to allow the Soviets to continue full tilt their program of MIRVing their ICBMs, the modernization program of highest priority to the Soviets and of greatest concern to the United States.

After Carter became president in 1977, the administration soon made two new SALT proposals designed in part to deal with the high levels of ICBM MIRVing permitted by the Vladivostok Agreement. In the most prominent one (the Comprehensive Proposal), the Carter administration proposed deep cuts in the arsenals of both sides. A key U.S. objective was to hold the total of Soviet MIRVed ICBMs at a level well below that which would threaten the survivability of U.S. ICBMs.

This proposal contained several changes compared with the Vladivostok Agreement. The total number of strategic launchers would be reduced from 2,400 to between 1,800 and 2,000. The total of

MIRVed launchers would be reduced from 1,320 to between 1,100 and 1,200. A new subceiling was proposed for MIRVed ICBMs of 550. A further limit of 150 was proposed for heavy missiles, a reduction from the 308 Soviet heavy missiles (none for the United States) permitted under the Vladivostok limits.

The Soviets promptly and publicly rejected the Comprehensive Proposal and pressed instead for U.S. translation of the Vladivostok Agreement into a SALT II treaty. In essence, this was what happened. The 1979 SALT II Treaty was, in effect, an improved version of the 1974 agreement with much more comprehensive limits than in the earlier agreement.

As signed in 1979, the SALT II agreement consisted of three major parts: a treaty to last until the end of 1985; a shorter term protocol which was to expire on December 31, 1981; and a joint statement of principles to guide subsequent negotiations. In addition, SALT II included a commitment by the Soviet Union on the issue of the Soviet Backfire bomber, an agreed memorandum listing the numbers of strategic weapons deployed by each side according to various categories, and a lengthy set of agreed statements and common understandings which set forth interpretations with respect to many of the provisions of SALT II.

The treaty restricted the United States and the Soviet Union to an equal overall total of strategic nuclear delivery vehicles. The units to be included under this ceiling were ICBM launchers, SLBM launchers, and heavy bombers.

Within this agreed ceiling, a number of subceilings were placed on specific types of nuclear systems. The initial ceiling for all ICBM launchers, SLBM launchers, and heavy bombers was 2,400. This ceiling was to have been reduced to 2,250 by December 31, 1981. Under these limits, the Soviet Union, which was at a level of about 2,520 in 1979, would have been required to remove about 270 strategic nuclear delivery vehicles from its weapons inventory, while the United States, which was at a level of about 2,060 operational systems in 1979, would have been allowed to increase its strategic forces slightly under the terms of the overall ceiling.

An additional subceiling of 1,320 applied to the total number of launchers of strategic missiles equipped with MIRVs plus heavy bombers equipped with cruise missiles with ranges over 600 kilometers. Within the 1,320 total there could be only 1,200 MIRVed ballistic missiles. Within the 1,200 MIRV subceiling, only 820 MIRVed ICBM launchers could be deployed.

Carried forward from SALT I were provisions banning the construction of additional fixed-site ICBM launchers with neither side permitted to increase the number of its fixed launchers for heavy ICBMs. These heavy ICBMs were defined as those with a launch-weight (weight of the total missile) or throw-weight (weight of the useful payload of the missile) greater than that of the Soviet SS-19 missile. The Soviet Union is the only nation that has deployed modern, large ballistic missiles of this type—namely, the SS-18.

The treaty placed a number of qualitative restrictions on the development and deployment of new types of nuclear weapons. Most significantly, the number of warheads on currently existing types of ICBMs was frozen at existing levels, that is, at the maximum number tested on each particular type of ICBM, as a means of slowing the expansion in the number of nuclear warheads. As a consequence, the Soviets were permitted under the treaty to carry a maximum of ten warheads on their heavy missiles—whereas without this limit, they could have deployed twenty or thirty warheads on a modification of the SS-18. In addition, SLBMs were limited to no more than fourteen warheads, the maximum number that had been tested by either side up to 1979.

Furthermore, each side was permitted to test and deploy only one new type of ICBM for the duration of the treaty. This exception gave the United States the right to proceed with the MX missile. By permitting the Soviets only one new type of ICBM, this provision was intended by the United States to inhibit the Soviets from engaging in a broad-gauged ICBM modernization program. The permitted new type of ICBM could be only a light ICBM (this is, its throw-weight could not exceed that of the SS-19), and it could not have more than ten warheads. In fact, however, the criteria for distinguishing the "new" from existing types were so permissive that Soviet ICBM modernization was not seriously affected.

Finally, the treaty contained limitations on cruise missile deployments. These pilotless missiles capable of being launched from the air, ground, or sea are of great concern to the Soviets. The United States agreed to limitations on its cruise missile program. The average number of long-range (that is, over 600 kilometers) cruise missiles that could be deployed by either nation aboard its airplanes equipped for such missiles can be no greater than twenty-eight. The maximum number of long-range cruise missiles that could be deployed on existing heavy bombers, such as the B-52, was limited to twenty. Any aircraft that was equipped with long-range cruise missiles was counted as an ALCM-carrying heavy bomber and was included in the 2,400 and 1,320 numerical aggregates.

In addition to the treaty, the United States and Soviet Union signed a protocol that was to expire four years prior to the expiration of the treaty itself. It placed limitations on certain systems with regard to which neither side could reach long-term resolution. First, the deployment of mobile ICBM launchers and flight testing of ICBMs from mobile launchers were banned. Development and testing of mobile launchers alone, however, was not restricted. Second, ground- and sea-launched cruise missiles with a range of more than 600 kilometers were banned from deployment. The 600-kilometer deployment limitation was designed to expire before the United States would be ready to deploy these systems in Europe or at sea.

The SALT II process thus consisted of three phases: the Vladivostok Agreement in 1974, the proposal and rejection of "deep cuts" in 1977, and the signing of the SALT II Treaty in 1979. Throughout this long process, Soviet bargaining behavior reflected a concept of strategic parity with three key dimensions.

First, the Soviets have seen parity as the sum of a series of disparities. The Soviet term *odinokovaia bezopasnost'* means "equal security for all sides." This concept is asymmetrical in that the two sides may have overall equal capabilities but each has the freedom to mix forces within this total.

The key asymmetry the Soviets sought to maintain throughout the SALT II process was the superiority of the Soviet ICBM force, the key strategic asset of the Soviet Union. In particular, the Soviets refused to cut back on their heavy missile program. Secretary Vance commented that "the Soviets had adamantly refused, asserting that their heavy land-based missiles were the mainstay of their nuclear forces and their counterweight to the large United States lead [in the mid-1970s] in the number of strategic warheads and to our technological superiority. They did agree in SALT I, however, to freeze the number of launchers of heavy missiles at 308."[11] Of course, the Soviets were able to maintain the same level of deployment of heavy missiles in the SALT II treaty as well.

Why did the Soviets wish to maintain a large force of SS-18 heavy missiles? One reason is the usefulness of the heavy missile in implementing a preemptive strike if war broke out. As a recent Carnegie Endowment report noted, "Giant Soviet ICBMs with highly destructive multiple warheads are the most effective means of delivering the biggest blow first."[12]

A second reason could be the significance of the ICBM to the Soviets in their ability to inflict unacceptable damage upon U.S. territory. The Soviets rely on their ICBM force as their most reliable second as well as first strike force.

A third reason for protecting the heavy ICBM is its utility in curbing the United States from conducting a unilateral breakout from the strategic arms talks. The Soviets accepted a ten-warhead limit on the SS-18 even though the United States believes this missile could carry twenty-five to forty warheads. This Soviet "reserve" break-out capability provides the Soviets with a useful bargaining chip of their own. Whatever the reason, the Soviets sought to give themselves the maximum flexibility to modernize their ICBM force throughout the SALT process.[13]

The second major dimension of the concept of parity embodied in the Soviet negotiating behavior was the desire to maintain a dynamic balance. Modernization was inevitable, but one could usefully bargain about the evolving parameters of modernization.

On the one hand, the Soviets hoped to create the most favorable terms possible for Soviet strategic modernization. Especially significant to the Soviets was the implementation of their MIRVing programs during the SALT II period. The Soviets deployed four MIRVed systems during the mid-to-late 1970s, namely the SS-17, SS-18, and SS-19 ICBMs as well as the SS-N-18 SLBM on the Delta Class SSBNs.

The inability to achieve a Soviet-style MIRV ban in SALT I (that is, banning the production but not the testing of multiple warheads of any kind) coupled with substantial U.S. leads in MIRV technology encouraged the Soviets to deploy an extensive MIRV program of their own. But after the Soviets were deploying MIRVed systems of their own they were ready to establish limits on such systems. The Soviets agreed in the SALT II Treaty to a limit on offensive strategic launchers, including a sublimit on MIRVed missile launchers at equal, although high, levels.

The Soviets were, however, willing to establish broad parameters limiting their own strategic modernization program. The Soviets accepted a fractionation limit (that is, on numbers of warheads permitted per launcher) on their SS-18 ICBMs. In addition, the Soviets agreed not to deploy the SS-16 ICBM, the deployment of which would have made SALT II impossible. The mobile SS-20 IRBM is a two-stage version of the mobile three-stage SS-16. The SS-20 was ready to be deployed in the mid-1970s as a theater nuclear system to replace the SS-4s and 5s. If the Soviets had deployed the SS-16, they would have been able to stockpile the third stage and, in time of crisis, rapidly convert mobile IRBM launchers into mobile ICBM ones. But in October 1977, the Soviet SALT negotiator Vladimir Semenov read a statement to the U.S. delegation at the SALT talks in Geneva saying that "the Soviet Union would undertake not to produce, test, or deploy its solid-fuel ICBM, the SS-16, or any component unique to it—that is, the third stage which distinguished it from the SS-20."[14]

On the other hand, the Soviets hoped to create the most unfavorable terms possible for U.S. strategic modernization.[15] At various times in the SALT negotiations the Soviets attempted to place constraints on all major elements of the U.S. strategic modernization program. The Soviets tried to deter the United States from deploying a new ICBM, the MX. The Soviets went so far as to suggest a total ban—with no exemptions—on the deployment of new types of ICBMs for the entire period.[16] The United States, however, saw the MX as necessary to offset the SS-18 and SS-19 threat and was unwilling to accept such a proposal.

Similarly, the Soviets hoped to curtail the U.S. Trident program. The Soviets proposed a series of "new-types" bans for SLBMs that would prohibit Trident I and II as well as the Soviet Typhoon SLBM but permit the new Soviet SLBM, the SS-N-8, or permit Trident I, SS-N-18, and Typhoon but prohibit Trident II. The United States would clearly not accept such proposals and the American negotiators argued that the SS-N-8 was analogous to the Trident I. Furthermore, the United States warned the Soviets that if they went ahead with the new Typhoon program, the United States would feel free to proceed with its Trident II program. In the end, both sides agreed to restrict the new-types ban in the treaty only to ICBMs. The only limit was on the numbers of warheads per SLBM launcher. During the treaty period, no SLBM could be deployed with more than fourteen warheads.

Above all else, it was, however, the U.S. cruise missile program that the Soviets wished to constrain. Strategic cruise missiles (eventually defined for SALT purposes as missiles with ranges greater than 600 kilometers) were a subject of great controversy throughout the SALT II negotiations. The Soviet Union argued from 1974 until 1978 that each air-launched cruise missile be counted as one unit under the overall ceiling on numbers of strategic launch vehicles. Eventually, the USSR agreed to include ALCM carriers in a subceiling category with ballistic missiles having MIRVs.

The Soviets also argued for a complete ban on long-range ground-launched cruise missiles and sea-launched cruise missiles (SLCMs). The United States would only accept a ban on deploying such weapons, or on testing them with multiple warheads, for a limited time period to the end of 1981 (a limitation included only in the protocol to the treaty). The Soviet Union made clear it would seek additional limitations in future negotiations. The United States agreed in the Joint Statement of Principles to negotiate on protocol issues, but made a unilateral statement regarding the need for reciprocal limits on Soviet theater nuclear forces.

The Soviets were trying to constrain the overall U.S. modernization program, the elements of which taken together would create a formidable threat to Soviet ICBMs in the late 1980s. As the Carnegie Endowment report noted:

> In light of their huge investment in land-based ballistic missiles, the United States's apparent determination to acquire a capability to destroy Soviet ICBMs must raise serious concern. Despite the erratic debate in the United States over the MX, the Soviets see a new ICBM, along with the hard-target killing Trident II submarine-launched missile, moving toward deployment later in the decade. Having dismissed for so many years American anxieties about the vulnerability of ICBMs, the Soviets have discovered the problem for themselves. They are also extremely disturbed about the American cruise missile program. Not only are the guidance and propulsion systems of United States cruise missiles still technologically beyond the Soviets' reach, but the United States has geographical advantages over the USSR that could make cruise missiles a permanent American ace-in-the-hole.[17]

The third major dimension of the Soviet concept of parity embodied in their negotiating behavior was an attempt to gain U.S. acceptance of the Soviet understanding of the equal security requirement. With regard to SALT, the Soviets have argued that the British and French systems as well as U.S. forward-based systems are part of the U.S.-Soviet strategic balance. The Soviet position has been that these systems must be accounted for in any "final" or "completely comprehensive" strategic arms limitation agreement.

The Soviets felt that the Vladivostok phase of SALT II provided indirect or implicit compensation for U.S. forward-based systems. Strobe Talbott of *Time* magazine characterized the Soviet position as follows: "The Soviets made another important concession at Vladivostok. They dropped a long-standing insistence that SALT II restrict United States nuclear weapons in Europe, the so-called forward-based systems. But this concession, too, had its price: the United States had to give up, once and for all, its dogged pursuit of a cutback in Soviet heavy missiles. This Kissinger agreed to do."[18]

During the 1977–1979 phase of SALT II, the practical consequences of the equal security concept revolved around the question of controlling West European access to U.S. strategic arms technology. The Soviets especially tried to push into the treaty a prohibition against the "transfer" of SALT-limited technology, especially cruise missiles from the United States to NATO Europe. The Soviets tried to apply a precedent from the ABM treaty to the transfer question. The ABM treaty contains a ban on the United States or Soviet Union transferring

ABM systems or their components to third parties. As Talbott noted, "The Russians wanted an almost identical passage in SALT II, forbidding the United States from "transferring" to NATO the blueprints or components of cruise missiles, particularly ground-launched and sea-launched ones. The three-year protocol already contained a ban on the deployment of long-range GLCMs and SLCMs, but not on their development and testing."[19]

The United States completely rejected Soviet efforts to prohibit the transfer of such technology to U.S. allies. Secretary Vance in his memoirs underscored this rejection:

> There was no question of our accepting a nontransfer provision. To have done so would have driven a wedge between ourselves and the NATO allies. . . . To ensure that Moscow could not misunderstand our position, [P.] Warnke [director of the Arms Control and Disarmament Agency] and I repeatedly told the Soviets that the noncircumvention clause was not a nontransfer provision in disguise, and that we intended to continue traditional defense cooperation with our allies after SALT II was signed. The theater nuclear force modernization decision and our decision to sell Trident I to the British are unequivocal demonstrations that we would not allow SALT to hobble traditional defense cooperation with our NATO colleagues.[20]

Although the Soviets were unable either to gain U.S. acceptance to count British, French, or U.S. forward-based systems in SALT II or to ban the transfer of strategic arms technology, the Soviets had not given up for good their long-standing demand for equal security. Rather, they had simply deferred it. This Soviet position was made clear by Brezhnev at the time of the signing of the SALT II Treaty in Vienna in 1979.

> President Brezhnev, foreshadowing political and strategic concerns the Soviets intended to address in the next phase of negotiations, said that it would be impossible to agree to new reductions until the sides had also dealt with the United States nuclear systems based in Europe and with the nuclear weapons of our British and French allies. The Soviets were increasingly apprehensive at the prospect of significant deployment of new, highly accurate United States long-range cruise and ballistic missiles in Europe which could attack targets in the Soviet Union. They did not intend to go very far in a new round of strategic arms reductions until they could take into account the threat against them from Europe.[21]

The problem of the impact of European-based nuclear weapons was becoming increasingly important to the U.S.-Soviet strategic relationship. This problem will now be addressed.

The Soviets and Intermediate
Nuclear Force Negotiations

The Soviets deploy three basic types of nuclear weapons systems for use in a European nuclear war—short, medium, and long-range theater nuclear weapons. Soviet short-range or battlefield nuclear weapons are designed for use in relatively close proximity to Warsaw Pact forces. Soviet battlefield nuclear weapons consist of artillery pieces (especially 152-mm guns, both the self-propelled and towed versions) and the short-range truck-mounted Frog and SS-21 (the replacement for the Frog) missile systems. Although NATO has a numerical advantage in battlefield nuclear weapons, the Warsaw Pact has significantly more short-range missile launchers in its inventory. As noted in one authoritative Western source, "The greater range, and consequently the improved target coverage and survivability, of land-based missiles more than compensates for NATO's numerical advantage."[22]

Soviet medium-range theater nuclear systems consist of dual-capable tactical aircraft and medium-range missile systems, the Scud B (and its follow-on, the SS-23) and the SS-12 Scaleboard (and its follow-on, the SS-22). The Soviets have steadily improved their capabilities for nuclear strikes with the use of medium-range forces. This has been especially evident with regard to the enhancement over the past decade of the nuclear ground-attack capabilities of Soviet tactical aircraft. The most capable Soviet tactical aircraft (the Fencer and the Flogger) were only introduced in the mid-1970s and began to be deployed in significant numbers only in the late 1970s and early 1980s.

The SU-24 Fencer is the first modern Soviet aircraft specifically designed for a ground-attack role. The 550 operational Fencers in the European theater have decisively strengthened the striking power of the Soviet air forces aimed at Western Europe. The Fencer is capable of carrying a large and diverse payload, including nuclear ordinance. It has the range to be able to strike most significant military targets in Western Europe.

Although deployment of the Flogger did not begin until 1971, it is now the most widely deployed aircraft in Soviet Frontal Aviation. There are two basic versions of the Flogger that are deployed with Soviet Frontal Aviation. The Flogger B/G or the MiG-23 is an all-weather counter–air fighter. It has become the primary air-to-air tactical aircraft of the Soviet air forces. The Flogger D/J or the MiG-27 is a ground-attack aircraft. The plane is capable of high subsonic speed at low altitude. Both versions—the MiG-23 and the MiG-27—

TABLE 5.1
U.S./NATO (Excluding France) and Soviet/Warsaw Pact Land-Based
Mid-Range Theater Nuclear Forces in Europe

System	First Deployed	Range/ Operational Radius (km)*	Number of Launchers
Soviet/Warsaw Pact			
Su-7 Fitter-A	1959	400	265
Su-17 Fitter-C	1972	600	688
MiG-21 Fishbed J-N	1970	400	100
MiG-23/27 Flogger-D	1971	720	720
Su-24 Fencer	1974	1,600	550
Scud-B (SS-23)	1965/1980	300 (350)	450 (10)
SS-12 Scaleboard (SS-22)	1969/1978	900 (1,000)	70 (10)
Total			2,863
U.S./NATO			
F-4	1962	750	172
F-104	1958	800	290
Jaguar	1974	720	117
Pershing 1A	1962	720	180
Total			759

* Range for missiles; average combat radius for aircraft, assuming high-level transit, low-level penetration of air defenses and average payload, unrefueled.

Source: Based on data obtained from The Military Balance, 1982-1983 (London: International Institute for Strategic Studies, 1982).

are nuclear capable. (See Table 5.1 for a comparison of U.S./NATO and Soviet/Warsaw Pact mid-range nuclear forces in Europe.)

Soviet long-range theater nuclear systems consist of a medium-range bomber force and an intermediate range ballistic missile force. The medium-range bomber force consists of the Tu-16 Badger, the Tu-22 Blinder, and the Backfire. The Badger (2,800-km. range) and the Blinder (3,100-km. range) are older systems but they are being upgraded to extend their service life. These older systems will eventually be replaced by the new Backfire bomber which was first deployed in 1974. The range of the Backfire (4,200-km. range) is significantly greater than that of the Badger and the Blinder. According to *Strategic Survey*, "This range allows [the Backfire] to cover all of NATO Europe, as well as large areas of adjacent oceans, from bases in the USSR; perhaps equally important, it gives the aircraft increased loiter time at shorter range, and thus an enhanced capability to seek out mobile targets."[23]

The Soviet IRBM force consists of the older SS-4 as well as the new SS-20 medium-range missiles. The SS-4 is a liquid-fuel missile which carries a single warhead. It is based in fixed-silo locations and

TABLE 5.2
U.S. and Soviet Land-Based Long-Range Theater Nuclear Forces in Europe
(December 1983)

	Missile Range/ Aircraft Radius (κm)*	Weapons per system	Total Launchers/ Aircraft	Total Warheads
Soviet				
SS-20 Launchers	4,400	3	243	729
Backfire Bombers	4,200	4	100	400
SS-4s	2,100	1	224	224
Badgers and Blinders	2,800–3,100	2	435	876
Total Soviet			912	2,223
U.S.				
F-111 A/E	2,000	2	156	312
Pershing IIs	1,800	1	9	9
Ground-launched cruise-missiles	2,500	1	16	16
Total U.S.			181	337

* Range for missiles; average combat radius for aircraft, assuming high-level
transit, low-level penetration of air defenses and average payload, unrefueled.

Source: Based on data obtained from The Military Balance, 1982-1983 (London:
International Institute for Strategic Studies, 1982); U.S. Department of Defense,
Soviet Military Power (Washington, D.C.: Government Printing Office, 1984).

hence is vulnerable to a preemptive NATO strike. The new SS-20 represents a significant improvement over the SS-4 in every dimension. The SS-20 is a solid-fuel missile, allowing it to be launched more quickly. The SS-20 is mobile and hence more capable of surviving preemptive strikes. The SS-20 carries three warheads which significantly expands the target coverage of Soviet IRBMs. (See Table 5.2 for a comparison of U.S. and Soviet long-range nuclear weapons in Europe.)

To reduce the military and political advantages the Soviets might obtain from their Euro-strategic arms, the United States in consultation with its NATO allies decided to engage in a theater nuclear modernization effort of its own. In December 1979, NATO agreed to the ultimate deployment in Europe by the United States of 108 Pershing II missiles (to replace the shorter range Pershing 1A) and 464 GLCMs, all with single warheads. The United States began deployment of these systems in Europe in December 1983, with deployment to be completed in 1988. The systems will be under U.S. control, although located on NATO European territory.

At the time of the public announcement of the decision, Britain, West Germany, and Italy committed themselves to the deployment of the new missiles. Britain agreed to basing 160 GLCMs, West Germany to 108 Pershing IIs and 96 GLCMs, and Italy to 112 GLCMs. In principle, the Netherlands and Belgium agreed with the deployment but did not publicly commit themselves to basing these missiles on their territory.

NATO's December 1979 decision also entailed a commitment to try to negotiate with the Soviet Union in order to stabilize the theater nuclear balance, especially with regard to the long-range missiles. From NATO's standpoint, the main negotiating objective would be to lower the level of deployment of SS-20s and to ensure complete elimination of the SS-4s and SS-5s. The West would use the Pershing IIs and GLCMs in part as bargaining chips to induce the Soviet Union to negotiate.

Prior to the December 1979 decision, the Soviets waged an intensive propaganda and political campaign in an attempt to stop the modernization decision from being taken at all. The Soviets portrayed the proposed NATO decision as an unjustified and aggressive action. The Soviets proposed in October 1979 to remove 20,000 Soviet troops from the German Democratic Republic and to offer to negotiate on a mutual reduction of Euro-strategic systems. Nonetheless, this proposal was conditioned on NATO not making a decision to deploy new U.S. Euro-strategic systems.

After the December decision, the Soviets initially insisted that talks could be held on intermediate nuclear forces only if the NATO decision was revoked. The Soviets indicated that the USSR could not agree to negotiations on its medium-range systems while NATO only intended to include in the discussions the new U.S. systems to be deployed in Western Europe in the mid-1980s. The Soviets maintained that a balance already existed between NATO and Soviet theater nuclear forces. The new U.S. deployments would upset the balance. They therefore insisted that any proposed talks include all Western nuclear systems of medium range on land and at sea, including those under British and French control. Marshal V. Kulikov underscored the Soviet position in the following words:

United States "experts" are resorting to the most varied tricks to prove the completely unfounded assertion about the USSR's upsetting the balance of power. Thus, for example, they omit in their calculations the United States forward-based nuclear means . . . and also ignore the nuclear weapons of other NATO states which could hit the territory of the USSR and its allies. We, however, must include the aforementioned means in our calculations because they are aimed at the Soviet Union and the states of the socialist community. They constitute the basis of NATO's nuclear potential in Europe. If one wished to make an objective judgement when calculating the balance of power, individual types of weapons must not be studied in isolation from one another but the nuclear potential of both sides must be compared as a whole, and this potential now is approximately equal.[24]

The Soviets are especially concerned to protect their Euro-strategic capability, for these systems enable the Soviets potentially to neutralize NATO nuclear forces in the event of hostilities. Consequently, to accept even a partial U.S. Euro-strategic modernization program has been perceived by Moscow as a threat to the existing "balance" and hence damaging to Soviet interests. As Boris Ponomarev, a Politburo member, emphasized:

> When the West began to draw up the "new nuclear strategy" and the program for manufacturing new missiles to be added to existing medium-range facilities, it was a threat to the parity of forces in Europe. In these conditions, the modernization of Soviet medium-range missiles does not make any essential change to the strategic situation, to the balance of forces on the continent and does not destroy existing parity. It is merely that some facilities are replaced by others, which are less powerful but more accurate. However, both [the old and new Soviet IRBMs] have the same objective: to balance the forward-based nuclear facilities in Europe or nearby.[25]

Nonetheless, the Soviets have been anxious to appear willing to negotiate as a propaganda weapon in the struggle for public opinion in the West and in order to prevent or to delay significantly the U.S. Euro-strategic deployment process. Also, the Soviets have portrayed themselves as more genuinely concerned with European security than the United States. As Brezhnev stated in 1981:

> The United States planned deployment in Western Europe of new United States missiles targeted on the Soviet Union and its allies is presented as a measure to protect European NATO countries. In actual fact this is an attempt to tilt in favor of the American side the strategic balance established by the SALT treaty between the USSR and the United States. At the same time, in case of a conflict the vulnerability of West European countries will of course grow to a great extent. In the meantime the interests of all peoples call for the continuation of the SALT process and the resumption of corresponding negotiations. The Soviet Union is ready to start such negotiations.[26]

During November 1981, both U.S. and Soviet leaders made public proposals for the reduction of theater nuclear arms that were based on very different assessments of the theater nuclear balance. For the

United States, the deployment of the new systems was necessary in order to *restore* parity; for the Soviet, deployment *upset* parity.

In his speech at the National Press Club on November 18, 1981, President Reagan said that "the United States is prepared to cancel its deployment of Pershing II and ground-launched cruise missiles if the Soviets will dismantle their SS-20, SS-4, and SS-5 missiles." Only with the complete elimination of this category of Soviet missiles would parity be restored. The "zero option" proposal included a requirement that all Soviet missiles of these types be dismantled regardless of their location, including those deployed in the Soviet Far East. The United States was concerned that the mobility of the SS-20 meant that moving the missiles out of the European theater would lead to their deployment or storage elsewhere.

Brezhnev asserted during his trip to West Germany in November 1981 that a theater nuclear balance already existed. The Soviet leader proposed, during an address in Bonn on November 24, that if the United States was prepared to accept a moratorium on deployment, the Soviets would not only be ready to halt the deployment of the SS-20s, but would be ready unilaterally to reduce the number of missiles in the European part of the Soviet Union. As part of an agreement the Soviets would be prepared to make substantial reductions in European theater nuclear weapons. In Brezhnev's words, Europe should become free of "all kinds of medium-range nuclear systems directed towards Europe . . . as well as of tactical weapons. That would be a real 'zero option'." In light of the evolving stress placed in Soviet military thought and force structure development on a conventional war-fighting option in Europe, it is not inconceivable that Brezhnev was making a serious proposal. The result of such an agreement would be, of course, to place Europe under the shadow of the threat of Soviet conventional military power.

From the U.S. point of view, the Soviets already had a six to one lead in European theater nuclear weapons prior to U.S. deployment of the new systems. In terms of long-range theater missiles, the United States calculated that the Soviets had 700 (including the SS-12 Scaleboard) to none for the United States. In terms of SLBMs, the Soviets had some thirty SS-N-5s deployed on Hotel Class submarines which were not counted under the SALT agreements. In contrast, U.S. SLBMs dedicated to European theater missions had already been counted in the SALT agreements. More controversially, in assessing the theater aircraft balance, the United States counted all of the potentially nuclear-capable tactical aircraft in the Soviet inventory directed at Europe as well as theater bombers. No West European NATO nuclear forces were counted.

From the Soviet point of view, a balance of NATO and Soviet theater nuclear forces already existed prior to the planned U.S. deployments. In terms of long-range theater missiles, the Soviets excluded their SS-12s but included the eighteen French IRBMs (SS-3s). The Soviets also counted the sixty-four British and eighty French SLBMs. The Soviets included all U.S. aircraft based on carriers, the British and French bombers, while excluding all of the Soviet tactical inventory. Most significantly, the Soviets included non-U.S. systems.

The United States and Soviet calculations reflect different strategic assessments. The United States has been concerned to make the NATO strategy of flexible response more credible by deploying a missile system that more effectively coupled European and U.S. forces. French and British systems do not play this role. These systems, although significant, are "last ditch" systems. Flexible response has been designed to deter or to end the war prior to the need to engage in the widespread use of weapons of mass destruction. The British and French systems simply cannot play the same role as do the U.S. missile systems in implementing flexible response.

For the Soviets, the U.S. systems are strategic, not theater. The new missiles give the United States more flexibility to implement a war-winning strategy. These missiles allow the United States to destroy Soviet military targets without using systems based on U.S. territory. In addition, the British and French systems must be included because of their increasing military significance. The British will bring on-line the Trident missile systems in the 1990s, and the French in the 1980s will substantially increase their numbers of warheads over mid-1970s levels. Also, if the United States could be forced to take into account these strictly national strategic forces, the Soviets would hope to undercut the political rationale in both Britain and France for having an independent nuclear deterrent at all.

There is an important contradiction in Soviet thinking surrounding the Soviet calculation of the strategic character of European theater nuclear weapons. For the Soviets, U.S. INF weapons are strategic in character whereas Soviets weapons are not. Defense Minister D. Ustinov articulated the Soviet position as follows:

The new American medium-range missiles are strategic weapons with regard to the Soviet Union. . . . While declaring officially that the new missiles are allegedly meant for the defense of West European countries, Washington in actual fact is intending them for the infliction of preventive strikes on Soviet ICBMs and other vitally important installations situated in the Western areas of the USSR. After all, the Pershing II missiles, which possess a range of 2,500 km. [authors note: 1,806 km. is the correct range] and a high accuracy, could inflict strikes upon the Soviet Union's installations at which they are aimed in just five or six minutes after their launch. This would substantially alter the strategic situation.[27]

Nevertheless, Soviet long-range nuclear weapons in Europe are strategic from the Western European point of view. The Soviet understanding of the threat to its security from the deployment of the U.S. Euro-strategic weapons virtually ignores the security interests of the West European nations. According to Moscow's point of view, the "correlation of forces" between the United States and the USSR on the nuclear level is what matters. No additional capability of U.S. nuclear deterrence to protect the NATO European countries against additional Soviet nuclear capacities is deemed legitimate by the Soviets. Thus, it is reasonable from the Soviet point of view for Western Europe to be exposed to the vastly superior Euro-strategic weapons of the USSR. This clearly seems the point of view developed by the Soviets to explain to Western audiences the nature of the SS-20 "nonthreat" to West European security interests.

Soviet military doctrine does not allow for a first or pre-emptive strike by the USSR. Even if we suppose that the Soviet Union is priming for a first strike (the "assumption" is completely false, though Western propaganda takes it for granted), it ought to be quite clear that in the present conditions any pre-emptive nuclear strike is senseless unless it destroys or at least substantially weakens the strategic nuclear potential of the other side's retaliatory capability. This the Soviet medium-range missiles cannot accomplish, because they do not reach as far as the United States and cannot hit United States intercontinental ballistic missiles. In the circumstances, a first strike in Western Europe would have no sense from any point of view, for it would only expose our country to riposte by an absolutely intact United States strategic arsenal.[28]

This position totally ignores the advantages such a first strike potentially gives the Soviets via-à-vis the West European nuclear powers which would, unlike the Soviets, characterize such a Soviet strike as strategic in character.

From the Soviet perspective, Western Europe has been living with Euro-strategic asymmetries to their disadvantage since the early 1960s without complaint and should continue to acquiesce in such a condition. But what the Soviets disregard is that the Euro-strategic imbalance of the 1960s takes on a wholly different character in the context of the attainment by the Soviets of parity in intercontinental systems with the United States in the 1970s.

In light of the competing strategic assessments by the Soviets and the Americans of the theater nuclear balance, it is not surprising that the INF talks begun on November 30, 1981, have been difficult. Until March 1983, the basic U.S. position had been the "zero/zero" option. The United States has offered to cancel the planned deployment of the GLCMs and Pershing IIs if the Soviet Union will eliminate its SS-20s, SS-4s, and SS-5s. The United States also asked for a global count of these systems in Asia. Finally, the United States rejected any inclusion of British and French nuclear forces on the grounds that the U.S.-Soviet talks are bilateral in nature and that British and French systems are not under U.S. control.

The Soviets totally rejected the zero/zero option at Geneva and offered more limited proposals. One proposal was to reduce the number of SS-20s located west of the Urals. This Soviet position would have allowed the Soviets to maintain a force of up to 300 SS-20s in the European Soviet Union. In early 1983, Yuri Andropov, general secretary of the CPSU, offered to reduce Soviet long-range theater nuclear force (LRTNF) missiles to a level equal to those of Britain and France. Andropov's proposal would have not required the Soviets to reduce or even constrain their INF systems in the Far East.

On March 31, 1983, President Reagan proposed an "interim solution" in which both sides would reduce but not eliminate their long-range INF missiles. The United States would deploy a number short of the planned deployment of 572 and the Soviets would build down to the agreed-upon upper limit for U.S. deployment. The president mentioned no specific ceiling. The United States continued to insist on global limits on counting Soviet missiles and on excluding French and British systems.

The Soviets publicly rejected the Reagan initiative. On April 2, Foreign Minister Gromyko stated that "if the position of the United States remains as now, as it has been stated, then there are no chances of agreement." Gromyko specifically rejected the global limits on counting Soviet missiles; he indicated that the Soviets would probably withdraw some of the missiles from the European theater to Asia and "install them on sites from which they could not reach Western Europe. This is our business and our right." Gromyko stated that British and French nuclear missiles are an integral part of NATO and that "it is impossible to close our eyes to them." He said it would be an "absurdity" to ignore them in the total account. He also insisted that U.S. carrier-based aircraft be included in any agreement.

In August, Andropov modified the Soviet stance in the INF negotiations. He stated in an interview in *Pravda* and repeated in personal letters to West European leaders that the Soviet Union would "liquidate" any Soviet medium-range nuclear missiles on its European territory that exceeded the level of French and British nuclear forces if the United States would drop its plans to deploy 572 Pershing IIs and cruise missiles. The new twist was the use of the word "liquidate" which appeared to indicate that the Soviet Union wouldn't merely relocate these missiles elsewhere on its territory.[29]

President Reagan responded to Andropov's initiative with a proposal of his own. Reagan's proposals were made privately to the Soviets but reportedly indicated a willingness to vary the number of deployed U.S. systems, especially the Pershing IIs, and to ease the total allowance of SS-20s in the Soviet arsenal.[30]

Andropov quickly denounced Reagan's proposals in very harsh terms. In the formal statement issued by the Soviet government in late September 1983, the Soviet leader argued that: "The essence of the so-called new move by the United States, which is being advertised as munificent, again comes down to a proposal to have the two sides agree on the number of Soviet medium-range missiles to be dismantled and on the number of American missiles to be deployed in Europe in addition to the nuclear potential already possessed by NATO."[31]

Just prior to the initial deployment of the new U.S. systems in mid-November, the Reagan administration made another offer to the Soviets. The key element of the proposal made in early November was to establish a "global" limitation of 420 nuclear warheads for each side on medium-range missiles deployed in Europe and Asia.[32] This limit would thereby allow the Soviets to have 140 SS-20s but would have legitimized an equivalent number of U.S. systems. The Soviets rejected this proposal too because their basic position was that no U.S. missiles should be permitted in Europe.[33]

In short, the two sides remained far apart throughout the negotiations in 1983. The difficulty in concluding an agreement has been rooted in the different interests of the two sides. For the Soviets, the Euro-strategic systems provide them both with a "nuclear firebreak," which makes the European conventional war-fighting option more credible, and with nuclear options short of an all-out nuclear exchange with the United States. Politically, the conflict within the West over the U.S. missile deployment serves Soviet interests in exacerbating East-West relations. These tensions have already reduced one major concern of the Soviets, namely, that the limited deployment decision of December 1979 might simply be the beginning of significant U.S. INF deployments in Europe.

For the Americans, the deployment of Euro-strategic systems is perceived to enhance the credibility of the flexible response strategy by more effectively coupling U.S. systems with European forces. By enhancing the credibility of the flexible response strategy, the United States is able to strengthen its political relations with Western Europe and to reduce Soviet influence.

Thus, it was not surprising when the Soviets walked away from the negotiating table in Geneva in late November 1983. But even though the interests of the two sides are deeply divergent, it is conceivable that some agreement might be reached. As NATO deploys its new missiles, the Soviets might become convinced that it is militarily in their interest to have as low a level of deployment as possible. But outside of this possibility, the probability of agreements seems low.

The Soviet Approach to Strategic Parity

The Soviet approach to strategic parity has been internally contradictory. On the one hand, the Soviet Union has sought political equality with the United States. To achieve this end, a static weighing of force structures, geographical situations, and alliance structures is required. On the other hand, the Soviets have sought advantages in technological competition with the United States, in part, through the arms control process. The political component emphasizes the importance of equality in rough terms whereas the technological dynamism of strategic competition seems to threaten any agreed upon definition of equality. The political component is static; the technological component is dynamic.

The Soviets perceive the strategic arms race as primarily driven by U.S. technological superiority. They are less willing, however, to recognize the important part that Soviet research-and-development efforts have played. Nevertheless, given the key role that modern technology has and will continue to play in the strategic arms race, the Soviets see strategic arms control negotiations as critical in restraining U.S. technology. From this point of view, "The Soviet Union's basic strategic aims have been to use SALT to protect Soviet strategic gains of the recent past and to improve its future competitive position. In this process, a subsidiary Soviet objective has been to try to contain particular United States strategic programs that Moscow has found most disturbing."[34]

To be sure, the Soviets have agreed to some technological limits on their respective programs. The Soviets have accepted in the SALT process limitations on ABM systems, mobile ICBMs (SS-16s), long-range cruise missiles, and orbital or fractional-orbital nuclear weapons systems. In addition, the Soviets have accepted a number of limitations on the upgrading of existing systems.

In spite of such limitations, the Soviets have tried to protect both the size and operational qualities of their existing forces as well as to provide themselves with significant elbow room for their modernization programs. As the report by the Carnegie Endowment noted:

In both SALT I and SALT II [the Soviets] have resisted proposals for substantial reductions in strategic offensive forces, particularly in systems where they have distinct advantages, such as heavy ICBMs. They have obviously considered heavy missiles out of bounds for arms control, since the United States has offered significant concessions in an attempt to bargain for the reduction of heavy missiles. . . . They have also resisted limits on the future capacity of existing systems, for example, the right to replace older missiles with new versions, to develop MIRVs, and to improve missile accuracy.[35]

The tension between the political and technological dimensions of strategic parity is likely to increase in the next twenty years as the arms race heats up. This is the focus of attention in the next chapter.

Notes

1. Gerard Smith, *Doubletalk: The Story of the First Strategic Arms Limitations Talks* (New York: Doubleday 1980), p. 94.

2. Ibid., pp. 94–95.

3. Raymond Garthoff, "SALT I: An Evaluation," *World Politics* 3 (1979), p. 17.

4. Smith, *Doubletalk*, Chapter 4.

5. Thomas W. Wolfe, *The SALT Experience* (Cambridge, Massachusetts: Ballinger Publishing Co., 1979), p. 15.

6. Ibid.

7. "V interesakh ukrepleniia mira . . . ," *Izvestiia*, August 24, 1972, p. 2.

8. Smith, *Doubletalk*, p. 91.

9. Ibid., p. 93.

10. Ibid., p. 514.

11. Cyrus Vance, *Hard Choices* (New York: Simon and Schuster, 1983), p. 50.

12. *Challenges for U.S. National Security* (Final Report) (Washington, D.C.: Carnegie Endowment for International Peace, 1983), p. 6.

13. This point is clear from both Vance's (cited earlier) and Brzezinski's memoirs. See, Zbigniew Brzezinski, *Power and Principle* (New York: Farrar, Straus, and Giroux, 1983), especially Chapter 9.

14. Strobe Talbott, *Endgame: The Inside Story of SALT II* (New York: Harper and Row, 1979), pp. 133–134.

15. See the discussion by Brzezinski, *Power and Principle*, pp. 331–340.

16. Talbott, *Endgame*, pp. 159–160.

17. *Challenges for U.S. National Security* (Final Report), p. 22.

18. Talbott, *Endgame*, p. 33.

19. Ibid., p. 149.

20. Vance, *Hard Choices*, pp. 97–98.

21. Ibid., p. 139.

22. U.S. Department of Defense, *NATO and the Warsaw Pact* (Washington, D.C.: Government Printing Office, 1981), p. 46.

23. *Strategic Survey, 1981–1982* (London: International Institute for Strategic Studies, 1982), p. 53.

24. Marshal V. Kulikov, "Interview on Warsaw Pact," *Neues Deutschland,* May 14, 1981, trans. in *Daily Report,* Foreign Broadcast Information Service, May 20, 1981, p. BB-2.

25. B. Ponomarev, "The most urgent task of our time," *Le Monde,* December 23, 1980, trans. in *Daily Report,* Foreign Broadcast Information Service, December 24, 1980, p. AA-2.

26. L. Brezhnev, "Talks with the Swedish Social Democratic Party Chairman in Moscow," *Tass,* June 12, 1981.

27. D. Ustinov in *Pravda,* July 24, 1981, trans. in *Daily Report,* Foreign Broadcast Information Service, July 27, 1981, p. AA-2.

28. *The Threat to Peace* (Moscow: Progress, 1981), p. 20.

29. *New York Times,* August 27, 1983, p. 1.

30. *Washington Post,* September 27, 1983, p. 1.

31. *New York Times,* September 29, 1983, p. 14.

32. *Washington Post,* November 14, 1983, p. 1.

33. *Washington Post,* December 18, 1983, p. 16.

34. Thomas W. Wolfe, *The SALT Experience* (Cambridge, Massachusetts: Ballinger Publishing Co., 1979), p. 248.

35. *Challenges for U.S. National Security* (Final Report), p. 9.

Conclusion

The Soviet strategic challenge in the 1970s and early 1980s has, we have argued, encompassed four major dimensions. First, the Soviet leaders have deployed strategic forces capable of inflicting assured destruction against U.S. territory and have recognized the "objective reality" of the U.S. ability to reciprocate. Second, Soviet leaders, while not anticipating a meaningful "victory" in conditions of all-out nuclear war, have developed a flexible military force structure in order to be able to prevail in a conventional war at the European theater level. They have also developed the military capability for the exercise of limited nuclear war-fighting options as well. Third, the Soviet leaders have perceived strategic parity to be difficult to attain in light of U.S. military and technological capabilities. Fourth, the Soviets have acted on a concept of strategic parity in the arms control process that has contradictory political and technological faces. Politically, the Soviets have insisted on an equality with the United States that seriously complicates U.S. relations with and obligations to NATO. Technologically, the Soviets have tried to use the arms control process to limit U.S. modernization programs while protecting their most significant modernization programs, especially their ICBM forces.

In spite of such contradictions, arms control agreements were forged in the 1970s. But will the political and technological contradictions of the strategic parity problem become so exacerbated in the 1980s and 1990s that the arms control process of the 1970s becomes an historical relic, something akin to the Washington Naval Treaty of 1922?

The answer to this question has three parts. First, how will the Soviet Union view the strategic environment of the 1980s and 1990s? Second, what are the likely Soviet strategic responses to this environment and how will the United States view the subsequent strategic environment? Third, given the conflicting assessments of the evolving strategic environment, what are the prospects for arms control agreements?

TABLE 6.1
The Strategic Environment in the 1980s and 1990s
(From the Soviet Perspective)

The Political Dimension of Strategic Parity	Western Strategic Programs (The "Technological Threat" to Strategic Parity)
1. Maintain equivalence with the United States.	1. Qualitative transformation of of U.S. forces (MX, Trident I and II, cruise missiles, and new manned bombers).
2. Maintain assured destruction capability.	2. U.S. R&D programs (Midgetman, stealth bomber and cruise missiles, strategic defense, and ASW systems).

3. Equal security
   a. Geographical asymmetries
   b. Third Country systems
	3.
	   a. U.S. GLCMs and Pershing IIs
	   b. French and British nuclear modernization.

4. Deny U.S. strategic superiority	4. Qualitative transformation of U.S. forces together with French and British modernization programs.'

The Soviet View

Table 6.1 indicates the Soviet view of the strategic environment in terms of the interaction between political and technological factors. A significant political dimension is the desire to maintain "equivalence" with U.S. central or intercontinental systems. The major technological challenges to equivalence are the proposed U.S. modernizations, namely, the MX ICBM, the Trident submarine-launched ballistic missiles, and the bomber/cruise missile combinations. Another political dimension is the desire to maintain assured destruction capabilities vis-à-vis the United States. The major U.S. technological threats to assured destruction are new ballistic-missile defense systems and the development of new technologies, such as the new stealth technologies, which will make it more difficult for the Soviet Union to destroy U.S. systems. Still another political dimension is the desire to ensure "equal security" with the United States. From the Soviet standpoint, two technological problems are critical challenges to equal security: (1) the United States capitalizing on geographical asymmetries by deploying ground-launched cruise missiles and Pershing IIs in Europe to gain strategic advantage; and (2) the West gaining strategic superiority through French and British nuclear modernizations developing outside the U.S.-Soviet strategic balance. A final political dimension is the desire to deny the United States the possibility of attaining usable strategic superiority.

The Soviet Union might well be wary of the qualitative transformation of U.S. intercontinental and intermediate missile systems together with the French and British modernizations that could enable the United States to conduct a limited nuclear war from Europe that would wreak unacceptable damage on the Soviet homeland.

The qualitative transformation of U.S. strategic forces will especially threaten the mainstay of Soviet strategic power, namely, the ICBM. By 1988, the United States plans to deploy 100 MX missiles in fixed silos. Each MX will carry 10 warheads of a new type—the W87—with an explosive power of more than 300 kilotons. The W87 warhead will be carried by a new reentry vehicle, the Mk-21, which has a much more accurate guidance system than the Mk-12a, which is currently deployed on more than 300 Minuteman IIIs.[1] The 1,000 MX warheads could hypothetically destroy almost the entire core of the Soviet ICBM force, the 308 SS-18s and 310 SS-19s. By 1998, the United States plans to deploy 20 Trident Class submarines, each with 24 missile tubes. The first 8 will carry the Trident I missiles, but by 1998 all will carry the Trident II or D-5 missiles. The D-5, which will be capable of carrying from 10 to 15 warheads, will have "the capability to attack all potential targets effectively from submarines."[2] The Trident force carrying a minimum of 4,800 warheads when conjoined with the MX force could be theoretically capable of destroying the entire Soviet ICBM force in a first strike.

The United States also plans to deploy at least 4,348 air-launched cruise missiles by 1990. "The extremely accurate ALCMs will be able to destroy the hardest Soviet targets."[3] The ALCMs will be supplemented by a force of 400 sea-launched cruise missiles by 1988. Not all SLCMs will carry nuclear warheads. In addition, the United States plans to deploy a force of 100 B1-B penetrating bombers by the late 1980s. From the Soviet perspective, the cruise missiles together with the bombers will significantly enhance U.S. second strike capabilities.

In addition to already programmed force modernizations, the United States has generated a number of programs that could further reduce the efficacy of the Soviet Union's strategic forces. For example, the United States appears to be moving in the direction of supplementing its fixed-silo ICBMs with a smaller, more survivable Midgetman.[4] In addition, the development of a stealth bomber would significantly increase U.S. ability to penetrate Soviet airspace.[5] The United States plans significant improvements in strategic defense. The navy plans to build a new class of attack submarines in the 1990s that will be larger, faster, quieter, and more lethal than the world's best nuclear attack submarine, namely, the Los Angeles Class SSN.[6] In addition, the United States has an active program in ballistic missile defense.[7]

The United States reportedly believes that "an active defense could protect some high-value strategic assets from ballistic missile attack."[8]

President Reagan in a major speech in March 1983 underscored the U.S. desire to develop an effective defense against ballistic missiles while reducing the threat of mutual assured destruction.[9] The speech has been followed up by Pentagon studies on the feasibility of "high confidence" ballistic missile defense systems. By the late fall of 1983, key defense officials were reportedly encouraging the president to adopt an ambitious ballistic missile defense research-and-development program that would provide deployment options, possibly by the end of the decade or, at least, by the end of the century.[10]

In addition to the challenges posed by improvements in U.S. central systems, the Soviet Union faces nuclear challenges in the European theater that seriously complicate its quest for equal security. The United States will deploy nearly 600 missiles with hard-target capability in the European theater. From the Soviet standpoint, these programs will enhance U.S. first strike capabilities as well as provide for a much more diversified second strike capability. France and Britain are also carrying out significant modernization programs. The two countries plan to have more than 1,000 strategic warheads by the mid-1990s. For Moscow, such programs challenge the credibility of the Soviet conventional war-fighting option or, at a minimum, clearly complicate Soviet plans to exercise escalation dominance in a European war.[11]

The Soviet Union might be confident that in the absence of widespread and effective U.S. anti-ballistic missile deployments, the United States will not be able to reestablish strategic superiority on the central systems level. Moscow must be concerned, however, with the technological challenge posed by Washington's strategic force modernization program. As Steinbrunner noted:

> Tacitly, the material pressure on the Soviet Union emerging from the Reagan Administration is qualitative in character. The apparent intention is to develop a more sophisticated, more diverse United States strategic arsenal rather than a larger one and thereby to force major adjustments in the large Soviet deployments. The implied purpose is to force the Soviets to waste the heavy investment they so recently completed by making it technically obsolete. (The most compelling threat from the Soviet perspective is the Trident II ballistic missile, expected to give the United States submarine force the capability to attack hardened Soviet ICBM silos.)[12]

For the Soviet Union, the United States could most likely reestablish a semblance of strategic superiority by enhancing NATO strategic nuclear capability in the European theater. The U.S. long-range theater nuclear forces when conjoined with British and French strategic systems, *even if numerically inferior* to Soviet systems targeted against Western Europe, would still potentially lead to U.S. strategic superiority, from the Soviet standpoint. If Moscow hopes to fight a conventional war in Europe, the British and French independent nuclear forces represent serious threats. If either a conventional or nuclear war is limited to the European theater, the discharge of U.S. LRTNF, British, and French nuclear systems could wreak substantial damage on the USSR itself. In fact, the damage could be so substantial that Moscow would have to terminate the war in order to preserve what remained of its state and society. Such termination would occur in this scenario without the use of U.S. or Soviet central systems. U.S. territory would remain intact. As a result, the Soviet Union might conclude that the greatest threat to the strategic balance involves changes in Western strategic capabilities in the European theater. Moscow might feel that derailing such changes by military deployments, arms control measures, and various political actions is a central priority in the 1980s and 1990s.

Soviet Strategic Programs

The Soviets have a panoply of central strategic systems under development with which to define their response to U.S. strategic modernization efforts. To begin with, the Soviets are developing two new ICBMs. The SS-X-24 is a large, solid-fuel missile, first successfully tested in December 1982. It is a medium-sized ICBM carrying ten warheads and is the replacement for the single-warhead SS-11.[13] According to *Soviet Military Power*, "The SS-X-24 will probably be silo-deployed at first. Mobile deployment could follow several years after initial operational capability is achieved in 1985. This ICBM is likely to be even more accurate than the SS-18 Mod 4 and SS-19 Mod 3."[14]

The Soviets are also testing a follow-on to the SS-13, known as the SS-X-25. A relatively small, single-warhead missile, it was probably designed to be deployed on a mobile launcher. Some Western sources claim that the SS-X-25 is actually a variant of the SS-16.[15] *Soviet Military Power* described the characteristics of the SS-X-25: "[It] is approximately the same size as the US Minuteman ICBM. It will carry a single reentry vehicle. The SS-X-25 has apparently been designed for mobile deployment, with a home base with launcher garages equipped with sliding roofs; massive, off-road, wheeled transporter-erector launchers; and necessary mobile support equipment for refires from the launcher."[16]

The Soviets also have an important SLBM modernization program in the form of the Typhoon Class submarine. The Typhoon carries up to twenty SS-N-20 missiles and has "design features that would permit [the missiles] to poke up through the polar sea ice to fire. Flight time to United States missile silos would be 15 minutes, or half the time it would take other Soviet warheads to reach United States targets."[17] Two will be operational by the end of 1984, with three to four additional ones under construction. By the early 1990s, the Soviets could have eight Typhoon Class SSBNs operational.[18]

Moscow is also working to develop a new long-range strategic bomber, the Blackjack A. This bomber will be used in multiple roles in delivering both gravity bombs and ALCMs to intercontinental range and is expected to be operational in the late 1980s. The Soviet ALCM program is closely associated with the Blackjack. As an official U.S. government source noted: "The Soviets are developing at least one long-range ALCM with a range of some 3,000 kilometers. Carried by the Backfire, the Blackjack, and possibly the Bear, it would provide the Soviets with greatly improved capabilities for low-level and standoff attack in both theater and intercontinental operations. ALCMs could be in the operational force by the mid-1980s."[19] The 1984 version of this report indicated that the new ALCM could become operational on the Bear bomber as early as the end of 1984.[20]

The Soviet Union also has several programs aimed at strengthening its strategic defenses. Its air defense is being enhanced by the deployment of new SAM systems (the SA-10 and SA-12) as well as the development of a new generation of look-down, shoot-down aircraft (Su-27, MiG-29, and MiG-31). Soviet anti-submarine warfare capabilities are being improved by the development of a new generation of SSNs. The Soviet Union is also pursuing ballistic missile defense systems. According to *Soviet Military Power*:

> The Soviets have developed a rapidly deployable ABM system for which sites could be built in months instead of years. A typical site would consist of engagement radars, guidance radars, above-ground launchers and the high-acceleration interceptor. The new, large phased-array radars under construction in the USSR along with [existing radars] . . . appear to be designed to provide support for such a widespread ABM defense system. The Soviets seem to have placed themselves in a position to field relatively quickly a nationwide ABM system should they decide to do so.[21]

The Soviet Union could combine these programs in a number of alternative patterns to deal with its growing ICBM vulnerability and to protect its strategic assets for second strikes. One response could be to maintain fixed-site ICBMs but to protect them with ABM systems. A deployed ABM system has the advantage of undercutting the effectiveness of the French and British systems. It has the disadvantage, however, of stimulating an "analogous" U.S. response that might actually erode the effectiveness of Soviet strategic systems.

A second response could be to maintain the ICBM as the premier strike force but to use mobility to enhance survivability. The fixed-base ICBMs could be used as the first strike force, with a mobile ICBM force as the reserve or second strike force. The development of a common intermediate range/intercontinental missile (as in the SS-20/SS-16 pairing) would provide the Soviet Union with a much more flexible weapons mix.

A third response could be to develop a more balanced force or "triad" of ICBMs, SLBMs, and bombers. The SLBM could emerge as the first strike force as the Soviets develop hard-target kill capability in their SLBMs. The SLBMs could then be targeted on U.S. ICBMs with Soviet SLCMs targeted against U.S. bomber bases. Soviet mobile ICBMs could then be used in a second strike role, with long-range bombers providing further countervalue coverage of U.S. territory.

It is more difficult for the Soviet Union to formulate an adequate response to its conception of the Euro-strategic threat posed by U.S. nuclear weapons. The Soviet Union already has a full spectrum of nuclear weapons deployed in Europe. There is no readily apparent "analogous" response to U.S. LRTNF that has not already been made. Of course, greater numbers of SS-20s, SS-21s, SS-22s, or SS-23s could be deployed in response to American deployments.[22]

However, the Soviet Union has an even greater difficulty in defining an analogous response from the standpoint of a similar capability to use tactical or theater weapons to strike U.S. territory. One possibility might be the forward deployment of Soviet bombers carrying ALCMs to Cuba in order to threaten the United States. Another possibility might be the deployment of a new class of attack submarines armed with cruise missiles that could pose a serious undersea threat to the United States. If the Soviets intend to use their SLCMs in a land-attack role, they could pose an especially significant threat to U.S. C³ systems and bomber bases. The closer a submarine can get to a land target, the less warning there would be of a cruise missile attack.[23] Soviet leaders will apparently focus on the forward deployment of SLCMs as their analogous response to U.S. deployments in Europe.[24]

Even more difficult to formulate would be a response to the modernization of French and British strategic forces. The Soviets already have a broad array of conventional and nuclear options to

TABLE 6.2
The Strategic Environment in the 1980s and 1990s
(From the U.S. Perspective)

The Political Dimension of Strategic Parity	Soviet Strategic Programs (The "Technological Threat" to Strategic Parity)
1. Maintain equivalence with the Soviet Union	1. Qualitative transformation of Soviet forces (SS-X-24, PL-5, Typhoon, Backfire-Blackjack/ cruise missile combination).
2. Maintain assured destruction capability.	2. R&D in ABM and strategic air-defense systems.
3. Maintain extended deterrence capability.	3. SS-20, SS-21, SS-22, and SS-23 deployments and their follow-on systems.
4. Deny Soviet military superiority.	4. Soviet conventional "superiority" in the Eurasian landmass combined with the qualitative transformation of Soviet nuclear forces.

deal with British and French systems. New systems, as opposed to augmenting the capabilities of existing systems, seem unnecessary. From the strategic standpoint, Moscow could implement a policy that would treat the use of British and/or French strategic weapons against Soviet territory as if they were U.S. From a political standpoint, however, the Soviet leaders will continue to follow a policy of trying to exacerbate diplomatic relations among the Western allies in peacetime in the hope that serious disunity would be evident in wartime. In a wartime setting such disunity would allow the Soviet Union the possibility of reaching separate war termination agreements with each major Western power at the expense of the others.

The U.S. View

The significant array of strategic programs that the Soviet Union has under development and its concomitant possibilities for alternative deployment mixes create a challenging strategic environment for the United States (see Table 6.2). The first political dimension, to maintain equivalence with the Soviet Union, is threatened by the qualitative transformation of Soviet forces. U.S. C^3 systems and bomber forces are especially threatened by Soviet SLBM and SLCM modernizations. In addition, the deployment of mobile ICBMs, if the United States is unable to respond for domestic reasons, might be especially challenging to U.S. targeting requirements. The second political dimension, to maintain assured destruction capability, is threatened by continued improvements in Soviet ABM and strategic air defense systems, especially if the Soviets decide to deploy a significant number of advanced ABM systems. The recent discovery by the United States of a probable ABM radar system in violation of the 1972 agreement raises such a prospect.[25] The third political dimension requires that the United States maintain a credible extended deterrence capability, that is, have sufficient nuclear forces to protect Western European as well as U.S. territory. The SS-20, SS-21, SS-22, and SS-23 deployments are especially threatening to the credibility of extended deterrence.[26] The fourth political dimension requires that the United States deny the Soviet Union the ability to attain military superiority. Especially threatening in this regard has been the Soviet effort to maintain conventional superiority in the Eurasian landmass while continuing to transform qualitatively their nuclear forces, both intercontinental and intermediate.

In light of the projected U.S. and Soviet assessments of the evolving strategic environment, will there continue to be significant opportunities for superpower arms control agreements? From the structure of the two assessments, the greatest probability for agreements seems to lie in the first two dimensions, namely, trying to maintain equivalence and assured destruction capabilities. Purely from a military-planning perspective, it would seem useful to have agreements to provide parameters to guide the modernization or qualitative transformation process. For example, one Reagan administration official in describing the threat to the United States inherent in the shift of the Soviets to a mobile ICBM in the years ahead stated that: "Whether mobile weapons ever represent less of a threat than today's weapons depends upon the total number of warheads allowed on each side."[27] In other words, without controlling the number of deployed warheads, mobile ICBMs might well increase, rather than decrease, the Soviet threat to the United States.

It will remain useful to bargain about what constitutes equivalence, especially with regard to intercontinental strategic systems. The assured destruction dimension will be threatened by changing strategic defensive capabilities—ABM, anti-air, and ASW. ABM systems remain the area of greatest possibility for limitation, even if the 1972 agreements are modified to permit more possibility for ICBM protection, thereby obviating the need to go to mobile ICBMs. But if there are no controls on the numbers of warheads, ABM systems might well be rendered inefficacious.[28]

The least likely area for agreement involves resolving the inter-mediate nuclear forces problem in Europe. The United States wishes the Soviet Union to recognize, in effect, the Soviet threat to "extended deterrence" posed by Soviet INF systems. The Soviet Union, in turn, wishes the United States to recognize the U.S. and Western European threat to "equal security."

Thus, the Soviet approach to arms control in the 1980s will probably embody several objectives. Although the contours of the U.S. strategic modernization program are increasingly clear, the Soviet Union will hope to control the number of deployed U.S. systems. For example, the U.S. Air Force appears to consider the plan to deploy 100 MXs as only a first step in a plan to deploy 200 of these missiles.[29] The Soviet Union clearly wants to limit the number of MXs deployed, and an arms control agreement would be useful in this regard. Moscow is also interested in protecting its strategic modernization program from technological obsolescence by controlling as much as possible the introduction of new technologically advanced systems in the U.S. inventory, but the experience of the 1970s should make the Soviet Union less than sanguine in this regard. Finally, the Soviet Union will try to gain Western acceptance of the equal security concept whereby Soviet nuclear capability would be weighed against U.S., French, and British systems as a totality.

The arms control approach of the Reagan administration has separated the problem of limiting intercontinental from intermediate systems. Although there have been solid political reasons to separate the two forums, strategic and intermediate, there will be significant technological pressure to merge them when the Soviet Union begins to deploy mobile ICBMs. It would be politically and militarily ques-tionable for any U.S. administration to leave uncounted mobile two-stage IRBMs while counting mobile three-stage ICBMs, for there would be obvious potential interchangeability between the two. In addition, as a general rule, incorporating intermediate forces into the Strategic Arms Reduction Talks would expand the scope of possible trade-offs.[30]

At U.S.-Soviet START which began in 1982, the United States has made a number of proposals aimed at controlling the process of modernizing intermediate strategic systems. On May 9, 1982, President Reagan indicated that the United States sought a two-phase reduction in strategic arms. In the first phase, land- and sea-based ballistic missiles would be reduced to 850 on each side. Warheads for these missiles would be limited to 5,000, of which no more than 2,500 could be deployed on ICBMs. In the second phase, the United States would consider limits on other systems, including long-range bombers and cruise missiles.[31]

The key rationale for the U.S. proposal was to halt and reverse the destabilizing growth in ballistic missile warhead numbers. The United States has been especially concerned with the heavy missiles, the SS-18s, and prefers a "deep cuts" approach to achieving equivalence in intercontinental systems. The U.S. position was modified, however, in June 1983. The new proposal allowed each side more land- and submarine-based missiles (somewhere between 850 and 1,450 launchers) but would continue to limit the number of warheads these launchers could carry to 5,000 on each side. The United States also continued to insist on a sublimit of 2,500 ICBM warheads as well.

In August 1983, the chief U.S. START negotiator, Edward Rowney, indicated that progress in the START negotiations had reached the point where a preliminary agreement with the Soviet Union on guidelines for reducing intercontinental strategic weapons was possible. Such guidelines would include counting warheads rather than missile launchers, setting an overall ceiling on a number of warheads on each side, and agreeing on equality in total missile throw-weight or lifting power.[32]

But major difficulties remained. The Soviet Union proposed that all missile warheads and bomber-carried weapons be "aggregated" into a single total for nuclear weapons allowable for both sides. The United States, in contrast, proposed one limit for ballistic missile warheads, ICBMs and SLBMs and another for bomber weapons. According to a Reagan administration official, "The talks so far have revealed a major Soviet concern about the approximately 3,000 air launched cruise missiles with which the Reagan Administration plans to equip United States bomber forces."[33]

In October 1983, the administration introduced a version of the "build-down" approach to arms control at the START talks. Three proposals were at the heart of this approach. First, two old ICBM warheads would be destroyed for every new fixed land-based missile warhead, such as those on the MX. Second, three old SLBM warheads would be replaced by two new SLBM warheads, such as the D-5. Third, mobile ICBMs, such as the Midgetman, would be on a one-for-one basis. According to Leslie Gelb of the *New York Times*, "This would penalize modernization of potential first-strike weapons and reward modernization in the direction of submarine-launched and mobile missiles."[34]

The Soviets have been less than enthusiastic about Washington's basic START proposals. Initially, they proposed that the SALT II parameters be accepted with one major change, namely, the banning of ALCMs. After the new U.S. proposals in June 1983, the Soviets showed some movement from this position. They no longer sought a complete ban on new U.S. systems such as ALCMs. But the Soviets continued to reject any U.S. proposal that limited their ICBM force without limiting U.S. cruise-missile and bomber programs.[35] In addition, the Soviets have proposed that long-range nuclear weapons be limited to about 1,100 multiple warhead missiles and bombers for each side but with no special limits on the SS-18 or SS-19 forces.[36]

Garthoff commented on the reason for Moscow's rejection to date of the U.S. START proposals:

> From the Soviet perspective, the revised proposals are fatally flawed. . . . The advertised flexibility does not extend to the key provisions that made the Administration's original negotiating proposal fundamentally unacceptable to Moscow. These crucial flaws are not affected by the flexibility on total ballistic-missile numbers and are in fact made worse by the American plan to deploy the MX.
>
> The 2,500 warheads ceiling would mean a cut of more than half in the Soviet warheads on intercontinental missiles, while permitting an increase in comparable American warheads. The President did not go so far as to impose explicit limitations on missile throw-weight . . . but he kept severe indirect constraints on throw-weight that would require Moscow to reduce by two-thirds its biggest and best strategic missiles, the SS-18 and SS-19, while Washington could go ahead with plans to build-up its MX and Trident II missiles.
>
> Worse still, from the Soviet standpoint, while the proposed agreement would alleviate the vulnerability of American land-based intercontinental missiles . . . it would greatly increase the vulnerability of comparable Soviet missiles—which are the most important component of Moscow's strategic force. There would be no equality of sacrifice and no "equal security."[37]

It should be noted, however, that Soviet unwillingness to recognize the legitimacy of U.S. concerns over the vulnerability of U.S. ICBMs to Soviet attack is at the heart of the current U.S. arms modernization program. Although the United States is now seeking additional countersilo capabilities, it is doing so in reaction to Soviet force deployments. Because the Soviet Union has been unwilling to talk about the Minuteman vulnerability problem, the United States has concluded that its only recourse is likewise to threaten Soviet forces.

From a U.S. standpoint, Soviet insistence throughout the arms control negotiations of the 1970s and 1980s on protecting their strategic assets (especially the ICBM force) and on reducing the U.S. technological advantage has been, at the very least, troubling to the United States. Wolfe has noted that one of the core issues of the strategic arms talks has been "where to draw the line at which Soviet insistence upon safe margins of force levels would cease to represent legitimate compensation for technological and other asymmetries favoring the United States and would become a demand for unilateral advantage threatening to tip the strategic balance perceptibly in Soviet favor."[38] The United States is not about to let that happen.

In short, the strategic arms race during the next decade promises to make a determination of what constitutes parity very difficult. The Soviet Union is apparently unable to derail (despite their best diplomatic efforts to do so) U.S., French, and British modernization programs. These Western programs coupled with what the Soviets deem to be their appropriate responses will threaten to undermine parity as it was established in the strategic arms agreements of the 1970s. But parity will continue to exist in the form of mutual assured destruction, especially if the United States and the USSR do not engage in widespread deployments of ballistic missiles defense systems.

It is not clear how, or if, superpower arms control talks will effectively curb technological competition or channel the Soviet and U.S. modernization processes into some form of bargained equivalence. There is a real danger that technological competition will become so intense that the effort to define parity through arms control agreements will collapse. This is particularly true if Moscow is confused by U.S. rhetoric, uncertain of U.S. policy goals toward the USSR, and convinced that Washington is out to regain the strategic superiority it lost in the 1960s through increased reliance on advanced technology. An open-ended and dangerously unregulated arms race could well be unleashed.

Notes

1. *Washington Post,* June 28, 1983, p. 7. Information in this section on U.S. systems has also been taken from Thomas B. Cochran et al., *U.S. Nuclear Forces and Capabilities* (Cambridge, Massachusetts: Ballinger Publishing Co., 1984).

2. U.S., Secretary of Defense, *Annual Report to Congress, Fiscal Year 1984* (Washington, D.C.: Government Printing Office, 1983), p. 222.

3. U.S., Department of Defense, Chairman of the Joint Chiefs of Staff, *United States Military Posture, Fiscal Year 1984* (Washington, D.C.: Government Printing Office, 1983), p. 39.

4. *New York Times,* May 16, 1983, p. 15; *Air Force Magazine,* (August 1983), pp. 22–24.

5. *Defense Electronics* (May 1983), p. 15; *Armed Forces Journal* (October 1983), pp. 24–25.

6. *New York Times,* May 19, 1983, p. 17.

7. See *Science,* July 1, 1983, pp. 30–32, and July 8, 1983, pp. 133–135, 138.

8. *Annual Report to Congress,* p. 227.
9. *New York Times,* March 24, 1983, p. 20.
10. *Science,* November 25, 1983, pp. 901–902; *Washington Post,* November 27, 1983, p. 24; *Harper's* (January 1984), pp. 50–52, 54–57.
11. See Robbin F. Laird, *France, the Soviet Union, and the Nuclear Arms Issue,* forthcoming.
12. John Steinbrunner, "Arms and the Art of Compromise," *The Brookings Review* (Summer 1983), p. 8.
13. *Washington Times,* December 23, 1983, p. 4.
14. *Soviet Military Power* (Washington, D.C.: Government Printing Office, 1984), p. 24.
15. *Washington Times,* May 25, 1983, p. 5; *Washington Post,* May 12, 1983, p. 1; *New York Times,* May 12, 1983, p. B-9; *Washington Post,* August 19, 1983, p. 1; *New York Times,* August 20, 1983, p. 3.
16. *Soviet Military Power,* 1984, p. 24.
17. *Los Angeles Times,* June 26, 1983, p. 1.
18. *Soviet Military Power,* 1984, p. 25.
19. U.S. Department of Defense, *Soviet Military Power* (Washington, D.C.: Government Printing Office, 1983), p. 26.
20. *Soviet Military Power,* 1984, p. 311.
21. Ibid., p. 34.
22. *Washington Post,* October 11, 1983, p. 9; *Baltimore Sun,* October 26, 1983, p. 1.
23. Joel Wit, "Soviet Cruise Missiles," *Survival* (November/December 1983), pp. 249–260.
24. *Washington Post,* November 25, 1983, p. 1; *Baltimore Sun,* November 28, 1983, p. 1.
25. *New York Times,* October 5, 1983, p. 8.
26. Pierre Gallois, "L'Option Zero est Inacceptable pour l'Europe," *Geopolitique* (April 1983), pp. 104–112.
27. *Washington Post,* August 19, 1983, p. 1.
28. Paul Stares, "Reagan's BMD Plan: The Ultimate Defence?" *Armament and Disarmament Information Unit Report* (May-June 1983).
29. *Washington Post,* July 2, 1983, p. 8.
30. *National Journal* (October 1983) p. 2179.
31. *Washington Post,* June 9, 1983, p. 7.
32. *Washington Post,* September 21, 1983, p. 1.
33. *Baltimore Sun,* September 9, 1983, p. 2.
34. *New York Times,* October 5, 1983, p. 1.
35. *New York Times,* June 10, 1983, p. 1.
36. *Washington Post,* July 13, 1983, p. 1.
37. *New York Times,* June 12, 1983, p. E-19; *Washington Post,* June 27, 1983, p. 2; *Christian Science Monitor,* June 23, 1983, p. 1.
38. Thomas Wolfe, *The SALT Experience* (Cambridge, Massachusetts: Ballinger Publishing Co., 1979), p. 156.

Acronyms

ABM	anti-ballistic missile
ALCM	air-launched cruise missile
ASAT	anti-satellite system
ASW	anti-submarine warfare
C³	command, control, and communications
CBO	Congressional Budget Office
CPSU	Communist Party of the Soviet Union
ELF	extremely low frequency
EMP	electromagnetic impulse
FBS	forward-based systems
GLCM	ground-launched cruise missile
ICBM	intercontinental ballistic missile
IISS	International Institute for Strategic Studies
INF	intermediate nuclear force
IRBM	intermediate range ballistic missile
LUA	launch under attack
LRTNF	long-range theater nuclear force
MAD	mutual assured destruction
MaRV	manuevering reentry vehicle
MIRV	multiple independent reentry vehicle
MRV	multiple reentry vehicle
NATO	North Atlantic Treaty Organization
NCA	National Command Authority
NMCC	National Military Command Center
NORAD	North American Air Defense
RV	reentry vehicle
SAC	Strategic Air Command
SALT	Strategic Arms Limitation Talks
SAM	surface-to-air missile
SATCOM	satellite communications
SIOP	Single Integrated Operations Plan
SLBM	sea-launched ballistic missile

SLCM	sea-launched cruise missile
Snapper	Strategic Nuclear Attack Program for Planning and Evaluation of Results
SRAM	short-range attack missile
SRF	Strategic Rocket Forces
SSBN	strategic ballistic missile submarine
SSN	nuclear attack submarine
START	Strategic Arms Reduction Talks
TNF	theater nuclear forces
VHF	very high frequency
VLF	very low frequency

Index

ABM. *See* Anti-ballistic missile systems
Airborne warning/control system, 36,
  41
Aircraft types, Soviet
  AN-22 Cock, 20
  Backfire, 20, 21, 77, 101
  Blackjack A, 144
  Blinder, 127
  MIG-23 Flogger, 40, 126
  MIG-25 Foxbat, 40
  MIG-27 Flogger, 126
  MIG-29 Fulcrum, 40, 41, 144
  MIG-31 Foxhound, 40, 41, 144
  MYA-4 Bison, 13, 37
  SU-24 Fencer, 77, 126
  SU-27 Flanker, 144
  TU-4 Bull, 10
  TU-16 Badger, 13, 20, 126
  TU-95 Bear, 13, 20, 37, 144
Aircraft types, U.S.
  B-1, 99, 102, 141
  B-29, 11
  B-52, 49–50, 59, 60, 104, 120
  Stealth bomber, 141
Air defense, 4
Air Defense Forces (PVO Strany), 10,
  13, 30, 40
Air defense missiles, Soviet,
  AS-3, 37
  Galosh, 42, 43
  SA-5, 43
  SA-10, 41, 43
  SA-12, 43
Air defense programs, Soviet, 74
Air-launched cruise missiles (ALCM),
  49, 58, 102, 104, 120, 141, 144,
  145, 150
Air surveillance systems, 41
ALCM. *See* Air-launched cruise missiles
Alternate National Military Command
  Center (ANMCC), 51, 82
Andreev, V., 73
Andropov, Yuri, 134–135
ANMCC. *See* Alternate National
  Military Command Center
Anti-ballistic missile systems (ABM),
  19, 40, 42, 74, 94, 95, 96, 97, 98,
  99, 111–118, 141–142, 143, 147
Anti-Ballistic Missile Treaty, 3, 42, 74,
  98, 111

Anti-satellite system (ASAT), 40, 43,
  79
Anti-submarine warfare (ASW), 20, 37,
  41, 42, 48, 55, 56, 57, 74, 77–78,
  144, 147
Armed Forces, Soviet
  reserves, 46
Arms control negotiations, 5, 7
  Soviet interest in, 3
  in Soviet strategic policy, 2, 7, 17
Arnold, H., 89
ASAT. *See* Anti-satellite system
Assured destruction capability, 58–59,
  61, 93, 114, 139, 147
ASW. *See* Anti-submarine warfare

Baker, John, 33, 34, 36, 37
Balaschak, Mark, 41
Ball, Desmond, 40, 54, 81
Ballistic missile defense, Soviet, 42
Baruch Plan, 89
Batitskii, P., 74
Bellany, Ian, 42
Berlin Crisis, 17
Berman, Robert, 33, 34, 36, 37
"Break out," 87, 114, 121
Brezhnev, Leonid, 20, 65, 103, 124,
  130, 131
Brezhnev Period, 14, 17, 21–26, 67
Burlatskii, Fedor, 25

C³. *See* Command, control and
  communications
Carnegie Endowment, 30, 51, 56, 57,
  58, 121, 124, 137
Carter administration, 102–104
Carter, Jimmy, 103, 118
CBO. *See* Congressional Budget Office
Central Intelligence Agency (CIA), 44
China
  Soviet relations with, 17
  and Soviet strategic policy, 23, 96,
  97
CIA. *See* Central Intelligence Agency
Civil defense programs, Soviet, 4,
  43–46, 75, 77
Clausewitz, Karl von, 4, 5
Combined arms approach, 22, 71–73
Command, control and
  communications (C³), 19, 29, 34,

155